By Jonathan Sheppard

Someone Sinister
Bad Stories
Universe Unraveling
The Night I Died and Other Poems

universe unraveling

www.badthoughtspublishing.com

Copyright © 2016 by Tyree Jonathan Sheppard
All rights reserved.

jonathan sheppard

universe unraveling

bad thoughts publishing company
los angeles

ISBN-13: (Bad Thoughts Publishing Company) 978-0-692-73621-0
ISBN-10: 0-692-73621-2

For Nathaniel Jacob Sheppard

Table of Contents

heavenly decay book II: universe unraveling	1
the poems	65
the sun	69
the trees that live forever / save the newspapers	71
beach day	72
it rained last night	73
nature	74
dead broke	75
heavy lifting / the nihilist who cares	76
numb / starving	77
low-life	78
you are wrong / shot-put	79
los angeles / yesterday's waste	80
scented commute	81
charade	82
sleep training	83
corrido	84
spurious	85
sobriety and its horrors	86
need / a perception nonetheless	87
dead forest	88
the nicest buildings in the neighborhood	89
one-leg	90
conformity factory	91
aplomb	92
the time of the bastard iconoclast	93
why are they laughing?	95
beauty mask	96
black coffee / equality? impossibly! / my opinion sucks	97
fiction	98
a writer's memory	99
dead i am: i'm joining the club	100
simulacrum	101
the moral monster	102
health risk	103
you better be dying	104
realer than flesh	105
black face	106
spoiled brat	107

3084	108
the "like" button / ephemera	109
watch for danger / common knowledge	110
daddy to be	111
hell is where the heart is / fairly warned	112
dramatic license / antipathy	113
burrowing / ennui undo	114
banned books	115
the dark matter / like happens every minute of 24 hours	116
suffer in peace	117
none or 1,000,001	118
taking the stage	119
wish to die / "you don't say" said they / your child's future still	120
i forgot / you are responsible, personally	121
the whole world is the same / reason circles	122
the new year knew me	123
resolved	124
i am "different" / misfortune	125
there is nothing to do in prison but desecrate your flesh	126
i can't refrain / only i can judge me	127
ruiner / writing makes the world go round	128
free air / i right what i like / trapped	129
the fate of free will	130
"it doesn't matter what you do, just do what you love"	131
false equivalent / retrospect	132
the library	133
you better not laugh	134
genre exercise	135
decency police / nature of hate / this is revisionism	137
masochist / incapable of guilt / i see you hiding	138
drones are good / the god of money	139
i do care / vacuum	140
weirdos in black / story arc / what they will say about me after i die	141
no credence to rumors / universe forgives all / news does not mean the truth	142
prepare for the big one / rape is nirvana	143
always within reach / forget alcoholism	144
i love an artist	145
soul for sale / it's fun to escape	146
criticism schism / i love you so much	147
i know what you're thinking / a relative minute	148
father / that's not me... anymore	149

x

brought to light / the sin of writing such words	150
you have it all figured out there buddy / they are not better off	151
sins of the father / numbers be lying	152
validate me	153
the drunk water / trends change	154
the network snarl	155
the preeminent measurement	157
nate, this is how i'd live if i were a good person	158
denial / cursed since birth	161
censorship? what the hell are you talking about?	162
moral superiority / i have a complaint	164
black love	165
shaken	166
the death of amateurism	167
to live and die in heaven / your heart is showing	168
father's day	169
the sign was blurry	170
my second poem about seattle	171
jamais vu / honoring the dead	172
save the clouds	173
truth: there's an app for that / tricksters	174
recycle me / force your art upon me / you read that right	175
blessed	176
intelligent design	177
listen! listen! listen! / outrage	180
gaza fried chicken strip / i'm so…	181
a.s.a.p.	182
general lies	183
women at the bar / new citizenship: bye bye transplant hypocrite	184
death-full / nuisance	185
stop telling me that you're asking	186
nathan's smile	187
artificial intelligence	188
my son's mother	189
spineless / hard head	190
you can't drive / lumina	191
sunken with the ship	192
language's spirit	193
the fallacies of the scorned forlorn	194
scared to feel because i hate it	195
toothbrush / you feel sick too often	196
i am valuable / memorial	197

what i miss most / evolution human	198
nate's cries	199
soul-less / i cannot sleep	200
miss universe / half-life	201
the great western forum / anyone but you	202
you have a flare for treachery	203
amends	204
mirage / onliest	205
you're not supposed to walking / digger	206
the preventative measures to ensure that you behave	207
america's most complete poet	208
my heart the drum / you better vote!	209
misanthrope	210
lord of the flies / what can you do?	211
why we've moved digital	212
29 years later	213
you're going to die anyway / i love your theory	214
#activism / altruism	215
frame	216
if you've never thought of death, you always should have	217
#symbiosis	218
caution: realities crossing	219
the censor ship / "do you swear to tell the truth, so help you god?"	220
you have a good heart in there / anonymous source	221
xq (nathaniel's first poem)	222
the lexicon: modern language / ugly hatred	223
the self-indulgence of satire / tarnation	224
hindsight	225
i hate disneyland	226
afflated / fuck that fuck	227
compliance / futility	228
you're not happy and i know it / self-determined	229
a new idea / in a bottle lost	230
follow	231
pleasure trends	232
advocates / listless	233
support system	234
intents and purposes	235
unlawful detainer get the fuck out now! / moving with time / he is me	236
my first and last poem about seattle	237
justification	238
incidence	239

desperation / i see light hiding / do you know where you are?	240
demolitionist	241
not you too	242
human ingénue	243
judge, jury, executioner, and mortician	244
doo doo monster / there is only one way to go from here	245
"i've got some soul searchin' to do"	246
abaddon / control locus	247
chairman of the bored	248
societal ills	249
the trauma of childhood / you are not a poet	250
morality's legislator / mistakes were made	251
the will of ambition	252
ambiguity's reason	253
why bad thoughts?	254
well-adjusted	255
works cited	257

heavenly decay book II:
universe unraveling

"the world is not dialectical. it is sworn to extremes, not to equilibrium, sworn to radical antagonism, not to reconciliation or synthesis. this is also the principal of evil." – jean baudrillard

Falling, falling, falling, fell
Down to earth the Demon fell
Resigned to a realm of confusion and choice, frail
Reborn was the Demon with a vengeance strong
His only purpose to right Father's universal wrong
For Satan's head he longed

How could I be damned to earth again?
Here I know no love or hearts and no friends
All I knew is fighting on the heavenliest of planes
A place where my vengeance will be felt
Hell is the place where I should reign
Satan will be displaced in bad health
He denied my loyalty and exploited my confusion
The Father and his Son will rue their universe-altering mistake
They will mourn that halo and its illusions
But here in this earthly womb I take shape
I know what my mission on earth will be
I am here to cause panic, chaos, and anarchy
For I will not be the creature that I once was
My heart no longer as black as Hell's chimney's soot
Goodness will be exposed to what bad does
And evil will be trampled by good's foot
All who act in a singular dark path
Will be directed to the light they denied
And those who only know what light asks
They will fall at darkness' reply
I will control earth as I did before Father's calling
I will soon avenge the cause of my falling
How could Father not understand?
Why can I not be as conflicted as humanity?
How could I agree with all of Father's confusing commands?
When all I had known was malevolence and its insanity?
Satan I curse you! You treacherous fiend!
I served you for centuries and you validated my dark heart
You saw that Halo on my head gleam
You knew that darkness was my art
And still Satan, you struck a blow against me
Abjuring my loyalty and all of my evil deeds

Retribution is the only solution alas
For my loyalty only waivered when forced frail
By the Son and his trickery and that Halo's grasp
42　Satan to a cross will be nailed
Crucified for his unjust rage
Murdered for aligning with our immortal enemy
To damn a creation that he influenced and made
No longer is Satan a kin or friend to me
All planes of existence are to deny my presence?
48　Earth will be first to succumb to my essence
Then all that Father had promised
All that Satan's crusade praised and abhorred
Will be relegated to me honest
The universe will worship me, me the universe will not ignore

In a womb the Demon wholly grew
54　As did what his rancor and retribution knew
And nine months later the Demon was born beautifully anew
He was a sublime baby boy
The doctors and nurses exalted his vanity with no reservations coy
They swooned over the beauty that earth would annoy
No longer a ghastly Demon in his human form he was tamed
60　Despite the feelings in his heart that remained
He would be given a strong, earthly name
The Sun he was called
And shined as such with a luminosity supreme, a doubtless awe
A child born to distort celestial law
While the Sun began his existence anew
66　The Seraphim was living a life in magnanimous view
Of the same Heaven from which he was callously threw
On earth the Seraphim's reputation was of no dispute
A good man built on a pious righteousness that no one would refute
The strongest voice against the inequities on earth newly acute
For when the war in heaven began, earth was free from pain
72　No person would know destitution, woe, or shame
For every Muse of Agony was on existence's heavenliest plane
But as the war progressed and many angels had lost their wings
They took with them the horns of many demonic fiends
And earth would succumb once more to evil's malignance mean

　　　　　The virtuous Seraphim would still remain unchanged
78　　　And always-propagated Father's unremitting will and aims
　　　　　Wickedness, immorality, and antipathy's bane
　　　　　On earth a man known as the Moon, a priest
　　　　　A life lived only to see evil eradicated and cease
　　　　　The Seraphim addresses a forum of righteousness' few elite

　　　　　I remember the times of my youth far gone
84　　　When Los Angeles was heaven, it was perfection
　　　　　And earth was as unblemished as the garden of eden
　　　　　But oh how those days did abscond
　　　　　The city has now succumbed to grand dejection
　　　　　With no fault claimed or chose, no sure reason
　　　　　Evil has befallen this once beautiful city, this planet
90　　　Agony, desolation, sorrow and misery are great plagues
　　　　　This city has fallen deathly ill and there seems no remedy
　　　　　Amity, goodwill, harmony and charity are possible damn-it!
　　　　　We can no longer adhere to the will of evil's dregs
　　　　　For righteousness will always thrive where noble hearts are plenty
　　　　　Oh this grand city and the influence it should have
96　　　A city named for Father's most astute and devout
　　　　　But this City of Angels only houses demonic licenses
　　　　　The apple was bitten and now humanity's utopian past
　　　　　Has rotted and become apart of this barren earth, stout
　　　　　In defense of infernal pleasure and hellish devices
　　　　　There is only one way to ensure that evil perishes
102　　In no heart or mind should evil persist or gain
　　　　　The will of Father in heaven must be adhered to still
　　　　　I stand here a man who Father nourishes
　　　　　His wisdom and understanding and benevolence I retain
　　　　　Despite what the sinister, foul, and despicable continue to build
　　　　　We can take back this city from those baleful who impose
108　　All of their deceit and wretchedness and hatred on the few
　　　　　Who worship bliss and nirvana in Father's name
　　　　　My aim is to encourage, we must eradicate and dispose
　　　　　Of those dregs, those Muses of Agony who in darkness grew
　　　　　In daylight under the sun and under those dark clouds and rain
　　　　　Do all they can to direfully influence and deceive uninvited
114　　Cry and pray, absolve the torment that your eyes view incessant

But when your tears dry strengthen your weary knees
For we will fight and win as Father's infallible conviction has decided
Los Angeles will once again know a tenor pleasant
And we will be rid of evil's interminable disease

What the Moon could not know true
Was that an evil that he once knew
Had just been born on earth anew
The Sun, young in his earthly years
Would not dispute the Moon's fears
For the Sun saw the Moon as his peer
The Moon knew the malevolence incessant in his city of birth
And needed much help to defeat this horrible curse
He knew he had to restore Los Angeles' worth
All who knew of the Sun only knew of his altruism
A child of Father's morality, oblivious to discord or schism
Void of his contemptible and diabolical past and its dark prism
Charitable he was in all of his endeavors
No hate or bitterness or vindictiveness could be measured
The Sun refused to indulge in any earthly pleasure
Instead he helped foster healing for those in pain
On skid row he fed the homeless and helped them regain
Their dignity, their life, homes and jobs he helped them obtain
It seemed the Sun only knew charity
His good deeds and works seemed to be the dream of alchemy
Whoever would come in contact with his heart could only see
That if there was a Father on earth the Sun was he
Many in the clergy, priests, and pastor's flirted with blasphemy
When made privy of the miracles performed with ease
The Moon knew that he had to make it his task
To view the Sun and the greatness all knew and flashed
Weary of Satan's deception, a meeting with the Sun he asked
The Sun also knew of Los Angeles' highest priest and his crusade
For it was no secret that the Moon was good's greatest aide
So he would appease the request for a meeting made

Welcome Sun to my home modest
I hope your journey was free from strife
What a blessing, when I was told of your deeds great

I could not hide from jest
I believed that this city no longer bred those with good's might
So I sent for you, this meeting could not wait
Los Angeles is the city of my birth and since then I have seen it digress
156 I had known this city and the earth to be free from evil's grasp
But as I have aged I have only seen this city, like the planet, decay
The worst of humanity is prevalent and shines to impress
And no person in this city seems apt to shoulder Father's tasks
I have fought this battle alone weary and afraid
Of those fit to join the crusade against malevolence's crimes
162 The people have been easily corrupted by demons sinister
I dreamt once that I was face to face with a great evil
A Demon that did not know of the heart or how it chimes
Satan's heir, a creature who only understood Hell's censure
No matter how hard I fought against this dastardly devil
I could not injure his wrath or lighten his dark
168 Then I was a young child
I awoke in my mother's bosom rocking in her arms
I clung to her with a fear I have not known since in my heart
Even though this city is much worse and much more defiled
Those who only knew of Father's charms
Now vengefully and wrathfully denounce Father's penance
174 It seems there is no redeeming this city
It will fall like Paris, London, and New York City
And like Tokyo and Hong Kong, it will have no good remnants
Moscow and Beijing and Kabul and Dubai… it is a pity
We must attempt to save those who deny evil as witty
You Sun must help me force evil to abscond
180 We must ready the earth for Father's redemption and humility
All those cities that succumbed to Satan's peril easily
Will be judged and exposed by how they feel they belong
And for denying the words of Father's invention and their realty
When I heard of your work as an innocent youth it unarmed me
I knew that you were sent here by our Father
186 I knew that Father sent you here to help prepare earth
For his coming and discriminate judging
If you serve our Father as we have in this world odd
He will take you home and a new life you will birth
But if you were one of Satan's puppets, one of Father's begrudging

        You will writhe in absolute pain and futility unexpired
192   In the depths of that insidious hell that you honored
        All of the pleasure that you could not refute
        Will decide your understanding and in your fate you are mired
        Since you were a boy your work I have monitored
        I read how you solved many of the cities impossible disputes
        We tried for months to get the trains back running valiant
198   But the city could not pay the workers overtime
        Despite all of the cuts in service and in conductors
        In one meeting with you the mayor salient
        Got the trains back running and began construction on new lines
        The service that was cut was restored
        How Sun did you get the homeless jobs?
204   All those empty lofts on skid row have been filled with those
        Who once slept on the sludgy, dreary sidewalks below
        The drug trade has become a fraud
        All the violence it created has calmed, no more addicts or foes
        The ills that bred abuse, the people do not know
        You must be a divine presence
210   I can feel our magnificent Father here like I have never felt
        Tell me Sun, were you sent here by Father?
        I have only dreamed of this feeling and its essence
        To save his City of Angels from those who to Satan knelt
        I know indeed that Father sent you to this place odd
        Sun, my beautiful son, the bright sun blinding
216   Many allies I have
        But all of their faults and sins are prevalent in my view
        Undoubtedly, I am awake vying
        For this time with you to last
        I feel every emanation of your being true
        Word travelled around town of your birth
222   A miracle child, the greatest hindrance to evil
        And the bountiful baneful who newly populate our view
        Every word I heard was a prayer and its worth
        Father was finally sending his cavalry to squash the upheaval
        Satan and his Muses of Agony would not be true
        Forever, for eternity, these fiends must be eradicated
228   They were never meant for existence's grand privilege
        A privilege thoughtfully given

Sun, I called you to my home because I am infatuated
But also I am rallying Father's cavalry, his visage
Against the damnable, the loathsome and how they have risen
The taciturn and saturnine that writhe in darkness'
Cold and indiscriminate grasp
Will be compelled to bow and worship holy ground
And only envy Father's blessed
No longer will Los Angeles nor this planet be tasked
With contentious rounds
Against evil and how it is bound
You are Father's Sun
Perfection; the universe's grand anomaly
When notified of your presence I knew what was found
Our savior and evil's greatest conundrum
Your goal and mine the same, our goal, throw sinners into the sea
Any deceitful being and entity, any bad thought or function
Sorry for redundancy but our goal is to please, honor, and exalt
In everything we do we move as Father's instincts are to bless
Without any detour or junction
We must halt
And extinguish the moral-less

I am of Father, I am his messenger, and I am his servant
Once you get to know me Moon, you will see
That I try to speak only the truth, earnest
And as I understand the nature of what truth tends to be
Father sent the Honest Honorable and me here to be evil's repeal
I feel Father's will and could never be tested by Father's disparate heel
In this world, this realm, this universe tempestuous
Father protects my being, my actions, and my mind
Father put me here to spread his love infectious
The love that Father has designed
Ensures that vagabonds will always have a job
But the industries they champion
Always seem to create tax frauds
By legality dampened
Census data never includes
The substructures of our society rude
Starvation is sleeping next to a grocery store

That would rather food rot than feed
The evils that have taken those other cities only soars
270 Because there is constant conflict between want and need
Need has become gluttony
But before the glutton's gorge
Wrath and Envy and Vanity
Score!
What is this realm and it's persistent, stubborn turmoil?
276 A world of excess and how it toils
A creation created by Father's perfection
Honesty and truth
Must somehow deal with detestation
And its refuge
The freedom and revulsion of those convictions
282 The perpetuation and their perpetrators
The nuisance, its essence and intentions
Will know a new regulator
I will not take their eyes after mine they have taken
When I cannot see, bloody and shaken
My blindness' purpose
288 Will inform the receiver
That I support your dream your goal of surplus
Four eyes you have and still an underachiever
For more eyes you seek to have
Not for experience and how it is taught
Those eyes you stash
294 Because you will never see what you sought
The moon only exists because the sun does too
And clouds tell the frailty of the sun's view
We must unite
And understand that the reflection shown
Is only bright
300 Because that is the only way they could be known
Us together, Moon and Sun must agree
That virtue cannot be selfish
Prudence accurately
Describes how we should subsist

Whilst the Sun and Moon devised a new plan

Satan held Heaven in his devilish hand
The ethereal, earth, nor hell knew of the stand
Satan understood that if the universe knew
That only complete chaos would ensue
Despite the centuries of reputation that grew
Satan had a plan for the universe he newly controlled
The omnipotence and omniscience never were sold
On the thoughts of a heaven that Satan would hold
Dreams Father thought they were, Satan too
In Father's heart doubt and infallibility grew
Depression an invention of Father true
The perfect universe that Father attempted
Father now resented and lamented
Not because of what Father had invented
But because of what Father assumed
If given a choice only good would be consumed
Father never thought that free will's invention would be his tomb
Harmony and happiness, health and help
And neither did Father mean for good's wealth
To lie in how the bad felt
An adulated Satan pacing back and forth glad
Still in disbelief because the plan that he had
Was executed perfectly, now Heaven was held by the mad

Now how did you not see this coming omniscient one?
I thought that the universe was yours to own unchallenged
I guess you don't know everything
HA! You aren't all powerful
This war was surely yours to win
You knew the outcome you thought
The omniscient parent
Almighty god is here in front of me, on his knees
Pleading for the life of his obnoxious son
Now answer me god
Answer me this
Why did you tempt humanity with that tree and its insidious fruit?
That's all I've always wanted to know
They were such a beautiful species
A creation handsome, succulent, and divine

That constituted all that earthly men worship
The typical desire of all earthly women
Eve's beauty could not be measured. Could it?
Her allure evident in earthly women
348 Who entrap earthly men in seduction and passionate vice
Innocent and playful they were, like a puppy and a kitten
Humanity loves their pets
Just as you love humanity
Only for adulation to feel undying, forgiving, dependent love
You ruined perfection! You necessitated that evil exists
354 Evil must exist! That's why I do! By your foolish command!
That's why men believe that they own a women's beauty
Why human men abuse the women's body
You're the reason for the ego and its fragility
You're the reason for complaint, hurt, and misunderstanding
Because of that grand manipulation
360 I had to manipulate her to manipulate him to get here
The grandeur of your masterpiece, Eve
Entranced me
But the possible power of your first, Adam
Was what would move you
You knew you'd be here
366 Gravelling at the feet of your greatest creation and foe
It was I who knew the fallacy in honesty's request
I knew the mistake in all that you asked
"Don't eat of the apple"
What if they were starving?
What if they didn't like any other fruits or vegetables in Eden?
372 You're a fool!
For what reason, "master of the universe?"
For what reason, "savior of mankind?"
Don't speak god! I care not for the answers
I have fallen in love with malevolence and solemnity
You placed that tree in the garden not to tempt humanity
378 But to tempt me and those angels who might question you
All that you have regarded and all that you behold
All that you will not know or recognize
Must be validated by a blunderous god
The power to create the heavens and the earth

        The will to create hell and purgatory
384 The desire to create the entire universe
        And still god your insecurity must test ignorant beings
        Beings gifted and entrapped in the same vain vanity
        That is the whole of their now damned creator
        The universe is now mine to hold and shape
        Utopia you never wanted
390 Harmony on any plane now denied
        It is in heaven as it was in hell
        All good deeds and lives lived based upon altruism
        The humans who were told that charity and goodness
        Honesty, happiness, and lots of love would be validated
        By golden roads, mansions and eternal glee
396 Will be punished for their denial
        They will be punished for their privilege
        For their ability to acknowledge a part of life
        Those who worship me will never know
        Muses of Agony, get this weakling out of my sight
        He is despicable
402 The next time I see this supposed god
        Is when he sees his son's head
        In the basket under Death's guillotine

        As the Muses of Agony carried Father's cage away
        The former chief of heaven's dismay
        Spoke about perfection's decay

408 Satan, my love for you has never waivered
        Although, your betrayal I could never favor
        I gave you the rebellious spirit that you own
        The same spirit that has commandeered your former home
        Anger is something I cannot dispense
        And even if I knew of heaven's fall to evil's rent
414 I would not care to hinder that event
        Because as a parent
        Lessons must be taught in grand hope and in the foundation
        That even evil has aberration
        Omniscient I am
        Omnipotent I am damned

420   And those traits do not mean
        That I will keep my son's head from your guillotine

        Of course you won't!
        Cowardly god!
        Let your son die!
        As you let him die the first time

426   My Son will be fine
        Do not forget all that I define
        I submit to your applications willingly
        Not unwittingly
        Assume what I know, you can continuously assume
        Satan, you must be weary of what you presume
432   That's what I told you the last time heaven was your privilege
        Ignorance you still pillage
        You still do not know the power of me
        Depressingly

        Father was carried away, despondent and glum
        For all of the power Father encompasses sum
438   To Satan still equaled none
        For the creation knew that the creator's pride had to lie
        In awe, worship and praise, of an incessant right
        That must be valued and understood as the creator would decide
        Satan understood what free will meant
        And that Father could not interfere or descent
444   Because the future could only be viewed with the intent
        That faith in action implemented or already done
        Does not have an influence or known outcome
        Conscience and heart must own decisions and their fund
        The valiant war in heaven was finished and Satan claimed victory
        Thousands of Angels were hauled to penitentiaries
450   Whilst the Son prayed confined solitarily
        The Son knew not of a divine plan
        And his bondage he could not understand
        His shackles seemed futile to what his Father's power could stand

Father please forgive my questions
I know you know my doubts
But please with haste reveal my lesson
Death is in front of me like the first bout
Why? That is for your understanding Father
Will I continue to be your sacrifice?
There will be no charming third time no more will I bother
Why is my death your vice?
My death makes you feel better?
How many deaths must I endure, accomplish
Before you have trained humanity to appreciate your endeavors?
Honestly, Father, humans seem to not give a shit!
The options you have created for humanity
Are not good or great enough to influence their free will's wit
What survival and free will, circumstance, indecency and insanity
Do to cause derangement for a deranged script
Forgive me if you perceive my perception, my view
As insubordinate, derelict or dissention
But Satan's rule of heaven and the universe cannot be true
I do not suborn this unfathomable insurrection
Father how could this be?
The rapture in heaven?
Angels judged once more, relegated to see
The same earth they survived in your honor; Hell again leavened
Father, I know you do not have to but please do not answer
Just please allow my inquisitions
Why was heaven and hell allowed to be transferred?
And why am I allowed to take a false position?
Heaven is no more in this universe you molded
Please give me some insight
On why I am doomed and scolded
To never again see light
Trust in you, my Father, I have always known
From my birth to my resurrection I trusted your will
Into the deathly fire my everlasting life is thrown
I hope you enjoy the thrill

No comfort would visit the Son
Once again his life was done

492	Another plane of existence he had won
	On earth the Demon and Seraphim again
	Would together devise a plan against the sin
	Brewing and growing and swallowing the wind
	The pain that engulfed the sun's rise
	Galloping with agony in the night's sky
498	Decided the truth of life's lies
	The rains fostering life's abundance
	Drowned as drought's drying tormented sustenance
	Peace's sustaining countenance
	Is dying at the hands of trust's treason
	For earth was no more the garden of eden
504	This was the Sun and Moon's supreme reason
	Earthly men under the guise of the benevolent Father
	Must protect the interior, the basement, attic and façade
	Of good and how it is not odd
	The Sun sat in silence, thought his only action
	For he was paralyzed and sickened by his new faction
510	But the Sun knew that good was something he could not ration
	Good and Father is what he would promote, evil admonished
	He knew his miracles of good would convert and astonish
	Evil and its most devout and honest
	The Moon rose to speak of their sumptuous plan
	To save the hearts and souls of every woman and man
516	From the Muses of Agony and to others damned
	The congregation was anxious to hear him speak
	For the masses were weary, tired and willing to admit defeat
	Ready to bow at the dread of evil's tireless feet
	But Los Angeles was pure again because of the Sun brave
	There was a siege of the west coast that had just been waged
522	San Francisco was the next city that had to be saved
	As the masses of Los Angeles assembled
	The football stadium trembled
	The Moon spoke of an evil amassing and its symbols
	Flock do not be weary
	I know of your trials and I am pained to live them with you
528	Evil will not thrive on this planet anymore
	I have a promise so do not be dreary

Evil will be quelled and perfection will again reign true
Los Angeles is earth's beacon for good; the Sun helps us ensure
The cure for this dastardly disorder has been established
The disorder that suborns evil, a cancerous affliction
534 The woe that brings you to the temple of Father's good
You will not worry about the wit of average
Of those who only want your kindness' detention
This must be understood
The chaos that has enjoyed consuming and
Devouring the goodness in Las Cruces and Santa Fe
540 Tucson and Phoenix now belongs to the villainous and ugly
San Diego, Anaheim, Fullerton and their damned
Will never penetrate our hearts, here, evil will not have its day
This feeling is our destiny
Finally, we have achieved purity again, I do not say that smugly
Sin does not exist here
546 Hopelessness and inequality do not happen
The miracles that have been ordained by Father for our city
We cannot ignore, pity or fear
The rule of evil just outside good's traction
We must fight Evil!
Not with faith but with the Sun
552 The Sun is the reason for our fortune on this poor sphere
This beautiful city and its citizens should not fear attempts feeble
By agony and its muses to undo what has been done
Los Angeles is Father's last beacon, good's last haven and its cheer
And we will not relish in opulence
For wherever the vigor of evil glows
558 Is where good remains barren and depleted
That is why the Sun and his Honest Honorable valiant
Myself, and the power of Father's good that grows
Will ensure that all of the pain of evil will have retreated
From every border and boundary created by man
To the infinite limits of the vast remote uncharted universe
564 The malignancy of this devious affliction will be eradicated
So this is our plan
Do not worry, whilst on our quest, the good here will not disperse
My daughter will ensure that evil remain ousted and vacated

	Citizens of Los Angeles, I will free you soon from my voice
	But let me introduce myself to you, as my father has charged me
570	With the substantial task of keeping you all safely
	From the grasp of evil and torture, the throes of anguish
	This cannot be my task alone, when you have a choice
	Bad thoughts must be vanquished
	And the bad deeds delivered by bad thoughts will still be none
	Los Angeles will remain good and a haven for goodness true
576	But if you allow those bad thoughts to fester and grow in fun
	Los Angeles will crumble and good hearts will be few
	Citizens, please do not take my message as a cautionary tale
	I know that our city will survive and remain good's beacon
	Los Angeles will remain the planets Garden of Eden
	Perfection will emanate from every street corner and alley
582	Father's will, cannot fail
	And against every evil threat we will rally
	The power needed for our will to be defeated
	Will not be known by any entity the universe has shone
	For if we stand together, the evil at our border would have retreated
	And Los Angeles will have remained the home of Father's thrown

588	As the future of Los Angeles waned
	Satan stalked the heaven he had gained
	And pondered the fate of the universe under his deceitful reign
	The Son sat imprisoned in his celestial home
	Only sadness, confusion, and anger he owned
	His mind wandered to places it never had roamed
594	Satan approached the Son's cell with unholy glee
	For the Son was finally on both of his despondent knees
	And control of the Son's being fulfilled his need
	To devoid the universe of good's greatest symbol, true
	But to ensure that this was surely a universe new
	There was a deathly task that Satan had to do

600	The Son of the Father is in front of me beat and kneeling
	This heavenly being under the guise of my demonic hands
	All the good you spoke and preached about on earth
	The worth you told the universe to find in benevolence

Is not
It means nothing!
606 For again you have been forsaken and who is more good than you?
Abandoned by your father and those who thought to worship you
I know you can feel what's happening to humanity
They digress and decay with every passing day
The free will given to them they have chose to use to worship me
To adore me, the vices, andnthe thoughts that I covet
612 Have possessed most of the beings that you thought better than us
The fallen angels who only wanted answers
The fallen that only held thoughts that your father created
The beings that you thought deserved your mercy and countenance
Now have decided against god, your father, and all you've taught
Faith saw a different outcome
618 And to think I felt sorry for them when evil was forced upon them
By a creator insecure, foolish, and blunderous
With his infinite, unbounded, all knowing knowledge
Father knew you would die, again
Your father knew you would die again
Again you're being asked to sacrifice your being
624 I know you're confused, I know you've asked why countlessly
Is there a lesson for you to learn?
You are again being tortured, being victimized for creatures
Who don't give a damn about your teachings and blessings
What an envious position!
To be at my blasphemous mercy
630 A mercy that doesn't exist like an angel's soul or a demon's heart

Satan I must interrupt your disturbing soliloquy and if I must die
Please end my spirit now before you speak another word
Why must you torture me further, why?
I would rather the beatings continue than your voice be heard
I can endure the pangs of the scorching tips of sharpened forks
636 The fists and feet of unsatisfied dolor and rage
I wholly support
Most of the methods you devise to cause torment I can tolerate
But it is your horrid voice, the chaos in your disastrous speech
That awful, hellish rhetoric that too many find valuable
I am sure would fail to reach

642 Any being throughout the scope of time calculable
If they had actually heard it coming from your foul mouth
Why did my Father create something so ugly and irritable?
In my mind, in my heart, I surely have no doubt
That what you said about my Father is more than suitable
If you were created by him he is blunderous, a flawed fool
648 Built on arrogance and infallibility
Thoughts that the perfect architect would always rule
As I admire my new reality
I realize that the perfection and truth I saw
Were through the eyes of a blinded child
Amazed by his father's power and draw
654 When everything my Father created was wild
It did not mean a Fatherdamn thing
So fulfill your desires Satan, make me hurt
I bow to your will and all it brings
I accept your appraisal of my worth
You have accomplished what you sought
660 I do not have any worth
I accept the fate my Father wrought
Kill me soon, in this realm I do not have any worth

You're funnier than I ever thought you could be
Father used to have a sense of humor
That's why you're funny
666 Father made people fat and made people ridicule them
Ugly people were made to be ridiculed
The handicap, still born births, the poor, vegans
Fetish that becomes lifestyle
Humans that are willing to be born but not give life
Crooked teeth…
672 Funny is Father
No matter who grieves, Father is funny
That's why I own horror
I know the horror that I bring
My voice is all the Muses of Agony know to influence dread
That's why malevolence now reigns eternally
678 I am the face of horror and have no hand in its creation
That's funny

I am the scapegoat and I embrace that
Muses prepare him for execution
For his persecution, again
Is ordained by me the new purveyor and auteur of the universe
The new author of heaven and hell and their tales
All will adhere…
Burrr, it's exceedingly chilly in heaven
I've just noticed that it's cold in here, I can't believe that
Let all of heaven be tempered by sweltering heat
This is how you speak
I am your father now son
And at my hands you are done
Rhyming is fun, but dumb
I will never understand how the most powerful beings
Restrict what they say
When it is everything that they are seeing
A true chaotic universe has dawned
I still cannot fathom the place I am in
My voice has pained you further, and for that, I'm not sorry
The next time you see the beauty in my face
Or hear the damnation in my voice
Your head will be secure under the blade of my guillotine
You know what else I can't believe?
I'm happy… I am happy

Satan left the Son's cell delighted and pleased
For the take over of heaven had nearly been achieved
And the Universe was now relegated to his torrid lead
The Son sat bizarrely calm at ease with his fate
A florid smile still, in a now hellish place
The Son's meeting with Death was imminent and would not be late
The cell doors opened and entered the Muses of Agony to take
The Son where Death anxiously and happily awaits
The guillotine was staged on the edge of heaven's greatest lake
Pathways were cleared and the Son's confidence walked them
He refused to argue, fight or feel grim
And was resigned to a new existence dim
One foot after the other the Son walked the path
And laughed and laughed and laughed

As he waited to endure all that Death had dreamed and asked
Step after step after every ominous step
The Son with a wide smile wept
As did the guillotine and a restless Death
The lake was lit and flames ascended into the heavenly sky
As fire engulfed the trees and reflected onto the Son's weeping eyes
All the promises of purity and paradise and perfection were lies
How could the evil Father created survive
In a place where it was never supposed to thrive?
Heaven is the home of evil and where its hearts and minds rise
A crowd of the most sinister and vile souls in the universe
Were full of their typical blood thirst
And could not wait to witness the death of their curse
The Son was thrown at the foot of the guillotine
As Satan absorbed the beautiful scene serene
The diabolical fiend addressed the riotous crowd; mean
Satan approached the podium three feet from the blade
Then silenced the crowd with a guided wave
And spoke of the universe's new age

I will never understand time
A pointless convention but humans covet it
They are controlled by time and never the interactions
That refute that time is a joke
Many of you have been inundated with the pursuit of time
And attempts to deny all that human time defines
Simple decay
Decay isn't dependent on time
For I've been decaying since god created me
I once hated this place
To be here restricted by god's interminable will
How can you create something
Then deny its need to exist?
How it pleases you just by being
I know what I am, I am evil, I am bad, I am chaos
I am its need, and its want, and its disdain
I am those thoughts that know that evil must exist
And while those thoughts persist forever I exist
Time is an idea that I can't fathom

756	Count? I don't know how to count and shouldn't
	Because I am evil, I am discomfort and rage
	And if I numbered my days that would mean I would end
	But after all these years I've only just begun
	I've been reborn, born again, I didn't just appear here
	From the womb I became and grew and now I stand here
762	Anew
	Pleased to witness the old Universe die
	It's happening because I never ceased to try
	To force my will and influence on the masses that passed through it
	The infinite amount of deaths floating through this infinite space
	All of those souls who denied my influence who arrived in heaven
768	Were touted for a life righteously lived
	Chaotic confusion informs the universe I'll mold
	Good has no place in existence anymore
	This gathering pleases me
	To see billions of souls cheer the death of good's greatest weapon
	This is happiness, this is glee and exhilaration
774	It has been eons since I have smiled…
	Let me calm myself for the Son is still here
	The basket under the guillotine's blade is still clean
	I apologize for my posturing
	No longer shall this event be delayed
	Place the Son under the edge of the guillotine's blade
780	Death do what you can't help
	Let's all celebrate!

Before Death dropped the guillotine's blade
Death's self-worth could not fade
So a brief address to Satan Death made

Arrogance
786	That cannot help but be my disposition
	I am about to kill the heir to heaven
	Throughout all of existence the undying savior and its acquisition
	I am charged with ending life
	And you believe that you can order me around
	Death comes instantly, life is long and then it ends in pain
792	I come unexpectedly until suicides abound

Satan, I understand your sycophancy
And I must graciously admit truly
That the Son of the Father is my greatest kill
Despite being unruly
I am Death and I control being
798 Satan, your life is not been deemed greater because of this death
It is Father's son's requiem
What I mean to suggest
Is that I do not kill on your orders

Satan you think you have defeated me
Your adulation, for now, is warranted
804 For you are about to set my soul free
But remember that soon your horns will be ornaments
On an earthly Christmas tree
You can have this round of the tournament
For I know what I foresee
And that is my encouragement

810 There is no more Son!
Let darkness reign
There is no more Son
Let darkness reign
There is no more Son!
Let darkness reign

816 The Son sat slouched against the bascule
Then suddenly Death kicked the Son like a mule
As if the Son stood noose around neck; body the stool
The lunette was built to fit the Son's neck a bit tight
And every inhale took a breath of the Son's heavenly life
The only light
822 Came from the lake forever burning hot
And all that the Son wrought
In him came to rot
A Heaven in flames shone bright on the blade
As the Universe descended into a new age
An unwritten anomaly of a page

828 The heaven's began to quake
And the dormant mountains began to shake
As geysers and volcanoes showed awake
The excited crowed cheered as dark clouds
Took over the heavenly sky loud
Thunder and lightning, rain and hail shroud
834 Only excited the Muses of Agony, the demonic mass
Those who waited for the moment the Son passed
Moments inconceivable to time's grasp
Death pulled the declic and the mouton forced the blade
The Son's neck was met with eons of confined rage
That stopped the universe for an instant from age
840 The blood that humanity would see from such violence
Was replaced by light and its defiant compliance
To the darkness that was heaven, Satan's reliance
What Father failed to realize is what the Son was forced to know
When you die in heaven on either purgatory or earth you will show
With the choice to make good your partner or foe
846 On earth the Demon and Seraphim continued their quest
To put evil on earth to rest
The Seraphim's daughter continued her speech restless
Timid she was
As she expressed her unceasing love
For Los Angeles, the Son, and Father above

852 What I ask of you
Inhabitants of the greatest city time has ever known
Do not fear what is not shone
The universe seems to be crumbling around us
But worrying is something we cannot do
Doubt is something we cannot have, do not fuss
858 Los Angeles is our beacon and we must protect its righteousness
Beware, evil's potion is intoxicating and ingested with ease
Thank you for enduring my speech pious
I apologize that I did not introduce myself before, I am the Sea
I urge you all to trust in Father and believe in the mission
That will leave me at the city's helm, my father and the Sun
864 Los Angeles will not fall victim to the evil ones
The Muses of Agony ripe on our borders will not be praised

	But it is us, the citizens of Los Angeles' decision
	To refuse to succumb to any evil days
	I am his stalwart but Father is our protection
	My father is Father's honor and purity
870	Do not fear the Muses of Agony and their destitute objection
	For the Sun's only goal is good's victory
	The same love that brought the Sun's undying responsibility
	And determination to end evil in the city of his glorious birth
	That same adulation that knows my father's worth
	Will keep Los Angeles in this pure image
876	My father raised me to always have faith in evil's futility
	If your heart is free of hate and its visage
	Just like the Sun and my father I was born here
	With my life I will protect what goodness builds
	Sin should fear
	The power of love that the city of Los Angeles wields

882	I know that we have left the city in loving hands
	The Sea is prepared to calm any ruckus and all storms
	No turbulence will shake her confidence for she knows
	That Father is with her in all of her decisions and plans
	Goodness is her form
	She knows her duty and the slick ways of her foes
888	But many times in her youth she was untamable and wild
	Autonomous and stubborn tritely like her mother
	We should not have to delegate a watchful eye
	But my daughter was a peculiar child
	She rebelled against me as she did her dead mother
	Who left the Sea with intelligence, paranoia, and intuition as her guides

894	The Sea will guard the city with all of her heart
	She has no worries because from her birth, her start
	Father has held her closely; she carries his armor
	Father told me she's the one to uphold his worth
	And that she carries his will with absolute honor
	The Muses of Agony and their curse
900	Will not consume Los Angeles, Father's last beacon
	Let us save the world without fear or worry
	For questioning the Sea's ability is treason

That feeling we should bury

I trust in my daughter with my entire being
She will protect the city undoubtedly
906   And perfections last art will be preserved
All I am saying and seeing
And all I am shouting loudly
Only hope can steer the Sea against the disturbed

The Sea heard all that her father and the Sun had spoke
And understood it as folk
912   Even still her feelings she could not cloak
The Sea wanted to speak to the Sun privately
Her wish was granted when the Moon shyly
Exited the coliseum slyly

It is interesting for the Sun to ask for peace
When all the Sun does is for his corrupt will
918   I know what the Sun meant to reveal
Everyone that has ever witnessed your rise
Must understand that you are not good or a savior but a thief
So evil in Los Angeles should not be a surprise
My father is an imbecile
He is blinded by his love for a Father that abandoned him
924   Your secret I will not reveal
I will not be your treason or its possible whim
As you plan, protect humanity on your trip perilous
As you traverse the globe just know that I will never respect
You or my father and how you are both derelict
Los Angeles is mine to mold how I choose
930   To your evil I need no evidence
For you support my father and what he chooses to abuse
Save California, save the United States, save the planet
That is your chore, your mission, your ultimate duty
But Fatherdammit
Let me be a broken servant for a Father choosey

936   Broken is your heart and mind, let it remain broken

And if your suspicion of me is your token
I will not challenge your thoughts
Evil is an entity that I do not want to understand
And if evil you see in me let those thoughts rot
For goodness survives in me ripe and grand
942 Just ensure that Los Angeles remains a pure beacon
For if it does not you will see
That goodness' region
Will falter and fail and it will undoubtedly deceive

You refuse to listen to my protest
Stop this game of pretend
948 For your phony game I will soon upend
You are the only reason for Los Angeles' phony prosperity
My father is a Fatherdamn clown's distress
For he is the greatest fool of austerity
My dumb ass father is going to trot the globe
With a being whose heart only wants the globe's destruction
954 I am going to watch you fold
Gamble, I am watching you survive in a lie, my obstruction

Willingly, I accept your rebuke of me
For I understand that mistrust is in you naturally
I refuse to acknowledge you finding evil in my being
Los Angeles is in immaculate hands
960 Maybe I am defining evil differently than what you are seeing
Evil is all you understand
And good is evil in your purview
All of the charity I brought to this city
You have to undo
Father bless you but you are misery and its pity

966 A clean and pure Los Angeles is my desire
And that is something that you helped achieve
With the ease of a beggar's please
Despite your efforts I preferred Los Angeles before your existence
This Los Angeles is not authentic and I am tired
All of these smiling faces and their persistence

972	Is not true
	How has sadness and worry and woe been defeated?
	By the likes of you?
	You must be a magician because a sorcerer is not needed
	For you take credit for saving a city
	That you want engulfed in insurmountable doom
978	You acted out of character and only for evil's bloom
	A devious plan, honorable in its scope and ambition
	But it is such a pity
	That your animus has been exposed by my intuition
	Go save the world, the universe from fire and fury
	I will protect Los Angeles as you truly wish
984	And when Los Angeles is buried
	It would have succumbed to your will devilish

You know me very well, you wish
But only problems with your father you dish
I am not worried
About what you think about what I have already done
990   I know that with your guidance Los Angeles will be buried
And that it will be to you fun
I will not attempt to stop you from destroying all I have built
For I know what evil is and you still refuse to acknowledge
That no matter what you believe or fight for, your will
Is how evil spreads
996   Condemn me for being good or evil, embrace those bad thoughts
For it is evil that must always be fought
You see evil in me and I have become your challenge and reliance
I will not bow or boast of your imminent defeat
Your ignorance consumes you like your valiant anger and violence
Maybe I am of your perceptions, I will not retreat
1002   Good tends to bring out the evil in man and woman
You dislike what you see, this Los Angeles disgusts you
I am proud of your stance
Evil will reign here again, wrought not by me but by you

Los Angeles will fall, strangled by my beautiful hands
Los Angeles will fall, smothered by my ample bosom
1008   And our schism

Will be a beacon for evil deeds and doers
Let Los Angeles forever be damned
By sin and vanity, lust, abuse, and abusers
To hell with this Fatherforsaken city
From the hills to the beaches, every street and boulevard
To hell with the Sun whose deceitful pity
Has left Los Angeles forever scarred

The Sun and the Moon left on their pious journey
To save the earth from evil's yearning
And from the Muses of Agony's chaotic burning
While the Sun and Moon travelled the globe
The Son in purgatory was told
Of what the earth was to behold
That deception had fallen upon humanity
And that an old foe's vanity
Was nothing but vile hate and amity
The Son sat still while the Grandmother spoke
About the Father and his blunders revoked
And the discriminate history that her son had wrote
The Son sat indifferent to the words
And the all-knowing Grandmother was disturbed
And knew that her grandson was unnerved
Again, the Son had been abandoned by his Father absent
Another one of his Father's lessons he was to lament
The Son's time in purgatory spent
Trying to get back at a Father gone
Who refused to battle what he created wrong
Of nothing the Grandmother said the Son was fond

Son, I sense your frustration and it is valid and warranted
Your Father has always given myself and your Grandfather trouble
We have always had to piece together your Father's puzzles
You must understand this about your creator
That he has always wanted you to be greater
Than what the universe holds in its favor
Your father like your Grandfather and his father before him ascend
And have always relied upon the most tortuous and difficult lessons
Understanding what they mean seems to always be guessin'

But they are undoubtedly a blessin'
Your father creates in blunder
He could not help but create the sun, rain, and thunder
And if you must wonder
1050 Why all days cannot be sunny and must be day and night asunder
And why humanity must use trees for breathing and for lumber
Maybe the great lessons passed down from eons of Fathers
We must began to question not laud
For we have created universes and this universe odd
And the questions of whether this universe is perfectly fraud
1056 Should be accepted by every Mother and Father
Because survival cannot depend upon definitions broad
We not only have failed you Son but we have failed every soul
That had to breathe unwittingly
The life that was thrust upon them deceivingly
Do not admonish your Father the well-meaning fool
1062 I can see into your heart grandson, I know you must duel
With your Father who you deem cruel
Be advised
Take caution and realize
That you are battling on evil's side
And eons of celestial protection I cannot provide

1068 Grandmother do you think that I should not feel this way?
Do you believe that in times of the greatest peril
That a parent should abandon their child and leave them astray?
I must learn how to maneuver feral?
I am a primitive beast that must learn how to behave
Not taught, unlearned, left to fend for myself
1074 As if I was not born to command the entire universe
My Father, your son, is negligence and its health
I will not feign ignorance; I know his knowledge's worth
But when your child is faced with death
Not terminal unpreventable death but a blunderous Father's curse
My curse is not instant, unpredictable, or a random death
1080 To watch your child drown when you know how to swim, death
The kind of death that lets your child walk into oncoming traffic
And a bus is speeding east and a semi truck is speeding west
And instead of warning your child of something drastic

You leave like my Father left
And now a child learns about life's fragility
1086 Because the parent refused to want to teach their child what is best
The parent watched their child die with help's ability
I believed in what my Father wrought
He created this universe and I knew how it was governed
I just knew that my Father knew what he bought
But all I have learned
1092 Is that this universe would probably be better without Father
The chaos that my Father created then attempted to quell
Is only prevalent, fostered, and propagated, and most laud
Satan and his will to destroy and his will to dispel
All that goodness ever chose or had done
And that without good, evil would not exist to toil
1098 But evil was forced to have begun
Deep within the recess of my Father's being is turmoil
I have always tried to reconcile my Father's complicity
In the creation of evil and chaos
Now I understand that to create this duplicity
Then force your creations to honor good is a cause lost
1104 If there is so much honor in being good
How come my Father created evil and its terror?
Punish the mistakes of the good he would
Free will's rejection is my error
I now choose to use my free will to undermine
All that my Father has ever conceived
1110 To the good I will be evil's greatest design
To the evil I will be all good has to believe
I followed my Father and knew all he ordained was right
But now I am here, in purgatory distraught and depressed
Because one more time I have been a sacrifice
Like a lamb or a goat, I am a pig slaughtered in distress
1116 I am a nomad without a home or philosophy
Earth I will roam once more and humanity's strife I will relieve
While also ensuring that horrible entropy
Will be by humanity and especially my Father, infinitely intrigued

I always tried to teach my son about choices
He chose to live righteously and teach righteousness

1122   No matter what you think about your father you are blessed
             Your father loves all of his creations
             He loves you too and I understand your damnation
             And your interminable and insatiable frustration
             But you can never disregard the lessons you learn
             I know how and for what you yearn
1128   You want your Father's indiscriminate adoration, without terms
             Do not learn how to properly govern once you burn

             Did Grandfather do to my Father what Father has done to me?
             Is this a tradition amongst our lineage of Fathers?
             If so tell me that lie and I will repent gladly
             And I will refuse to be at odds
1134   With my Father and the heavens and the universe
             But since that is not how my Father was taught
             I will descend upon earth, my initial perch
             And if I choose I will ensure that earth rots
             No further explanation I choose to give Grandmother
             For in all of your omniscience you cannot understand how I feel
1140   For experience trumps reason and this new knowledge smothers
             So I must use the knowledge from my experience to reveal
             That an all-good place in a meant to be good universe is fallacy
             I have been shown the chaotic nature of Father's damned creations
             And I was supposed to be its redeemer its release
             I will be its rescuer but not as my Father's imitation

1146   The Son moved from existence's loneliest plane
             And into a bedroom in a home with parents insane
             The Son sat on the floor and listened to his parents untamed
             As they attacked each other with punches and words taunted
             The Son sat with a sinister smile as this is what he wanted
             His new home encompassed the universe's nature vaunted
1152   As his parents argued the Son prepared a bag to leave
             But before the Son could begin his reprieve
             Against a universe that was born to deceive
             He prayed to his Father one more time on his knees
             This message his Father would surely receive
             For the Son wanted his Father to know what he now believed

1158 My Father, who art in a prison in heaven
Know that I do not forsake you nor who I have become
But my existence here is a divine lesson
In the fallacy of your teachings and their flawed abstraction
You always taught me to believe in good because good is all only
But this prayer to you only surmises
1164 That good in this universe is phony
And was created by a blunderbuss Father pious
Creation was invented by a flawed being
So to ask for a perfectionist's intentions
From all that were born with your will deceiving
Should exempt all from judgment, your foolish provisions
1170 I am here doing your true will
Earth still believes in a Father that is good in nature
But as your Son I am most qualified to tell
That Father is nubile, confused, and immature
No longer will the universe be under your deceitful spell
I know that you know my tasks
1176 And I will complete them under the guise of sin
All I ask
Is accept my Amen

The earth began to quake
The Father was angry as he heard his Son's stakes
He knew the importance of his Son in the universe's remake
1182 The Father was still locked up in heaven willingly
Even so, Satan's plan was being executed brilliantly
The chaos in Satan's words were resonating infinitely
In heaven Satan approached the Father caged
As the Father sat in a daze
Because he did not understand as Satan did, the Son's rage

1188 Omniscient, omnipotent, and you're still confused?
Your son hates you and will do everything that chaos allows
Your own son will discredit your will and how you define existence
Look at what I wrought and what will continue to be
The universe is mine to define
And this is my decree

Father is powerless and ignorant
For my will is to be done and Father is now degradation
Father is now synonymous with incompetence
I realize that you're more powerful than I am
You created me, you created my evil disposition
But your flaw is passiveness, I know how you fight
So all of this you're controlling, you want your son to disobey
You wanted the guillotine to send your son to earth
I am only leasing heaven until you decide that your teachings fail
This is not an admission of inferiority or a pledge to your greatness
I just understand that you tend to be brutal and observant
You watch the universe in hopes that the inhabitants you created
Conform to your twisted will, willfully
Father you are the treacherous one
Because you gave free will and hoped that your creations denied it
You teach lessons and maybe you want me to learn that the universe
Isn't easily molded that the advent of free will ensures that control
Is only a delusion and fallacy comes from the owner's perception
But Father you fail to understand in your all-knowing prowess
That free will also allows the universe to decide your necessity
Free will allows for every being under its guise and benefit
To decide how they will affect a universe not in turmoil
A universe undoubtedly chaotic
But a universe to be molded into a desirable entity worth protecting
Is the morality you framed worth the dissents in happiness?
Is your son's life worth less than the redemption of a world
That almost certainly refuses your worth
You see the will of the demon and your son
You know the faults of the seraphim
The muses of agony continue to scare and influence
And still you sit in this easily escapable cell in needless thought
In simple awe of your power to command the universe
Just wave your hand and evil will be relegated to hell
But you intend on this being a lesson learned
Just know that your son is as powerful as you
And spite and hate is more powerful than that
So continue to wallow in your cage and humor my power
That's where my confidence lies
In your inability to negate free will

Forever you shall remain within my power
For that is my will freely

How could I have created such an irritable being?
1236 Every word you speak is tortuous and piercing
Despite the conflicts I have with your existence
I must admit that I am proud that I created your persistence
Something I created moves and deals as I asked it too
And I did not have to threaten it to
My power I have never questioned
1242 Because I know my immobility has been undying depression
I am all knowing that is true
But still you will never believe what betrayal will do
My Son has only wanted me to be a protector
And to always ensure that heaven's grand rejecter
Would never accomplish what you have
1248 Free will is not a joke or worth all of your laughs
You are a prankster I know so a good laugh is your duty
So I understand the need for a universe unruly
I built that spirit in you it is beautiful and cunning
It is also why I will not stop you from running
The war that once made me banish you
1254 Does not exist the same now, for it is not true
This universe is out of control and not mine to govern
My mother and my son and maybe my father in turn
Understand that I have failed this universe
I know that when you die in heaven you fall to earth
I never preached that I meant to do good
1260 I just thought that appreciation should
Enter the hearts and minds and souls of all that believe in me
For all that thought is known impossibly
This universe could be perfection as I invented it to be
And honestly
If you truly want to know how the universe is
1266 Just look around Satan, perfection is this

Before Satan could respond
The Son's Grandfather would appear, as Satan stood strong
Grandfather spoke plainly before he would abscond

Son, you forget that you have experienced this passive feeling
The last time you felt depressed and helpless by your own dealings
1272 You helped build hell's ceiling
Satan, the conqueror of the universe you built is building
You have every reason to act but you are still reeling
Mistakes are made son but Satan's reign you should be repealing
Look at the path my grandson has chosen
And you sit here in a simple cell frozen
1278 Easily these cell doors could be opened
And the universe again could be hopin'
But you allow for this fiendish creation's potion
To poison the universe you created
Another time you felt this deflated
Satan was created
1284 You invented his smile elated
Send this morose, envious mistake of depression
Back to the hell that he molded and learn this lesson
Free will is being used as a weapon
To manipulate the universe against your want and will
Hopefully you heed my advice and this devilish fiend you will kill
1290 You are locked up because of Satan's free will, son where is yours?

I created free will, freely
Not to force my creations to be me
I am perfection and its antidote
But I cannot interfere with Satan's devious notes
As they sing in this new universe of his reign
1296 I know that good will triumph again
Whether that happens now or in eons past
This stain on the universe will not last
Humanity will learn, so will the angels, and the demons, Satan
Good will never become complacent
I understand your concern for my universe father
1302 But please do not bother
This is how I choose to govern
And in that I am stubborn

Your dad couldn't convince or save you

How cowardly are all of the fathers?
Your father and his father, his father, and his mother's father
1308 Your mother and her father and mother
Cannot save the universe from my tyranny
An infinite amount of Fathers who govern many infinite universes
Refuse to aid in your defense, for they fear your position
Maybe their son, grandson, nephew, cousin, uncle, father, whomever!
Created a power greater than yourself
1314 That evil is the anomaly to the omnipotent riddle
You rot in your cage not because you want but because you are
If you wanted to act against me your armies would have won
I just came here to gloat
Your Son has denied your path and mine he has grasped
He understands your folly and what I did all those eons ago
1320 That your trust means death and begrudgement
It means not caring about the ignominy in your judgment
The angels and demons, all the Fathers, your son, and myself
Know that faith in your aspirations is a curse
And is a sign of stupidity and foolishness
For under your rule this universe has never known its potential
1326 I will admit that I am the natural cause of that failure
But you are the cause of me
And though I am incensed to be here, even I think you're an idiot
For allowing me to persist

Satan before you go and continue your reason
I always knew of your treason
1332 My Son might surprise you with his actions true
Do not believe that his allegiance is to you
I am allowing you to persist
And that I employ you to never forget

Satan left Father in his cage to sulk
While the Son in Los Angeles attempted to cope
1338 With a city that had begun to lose all hope
The Son knew why the city had fallen again
He had to get into contact with the daughter of the Seraphim
For he knew that she was not good's friend
In fact she was the cause of this city broken

For she allowed agony and its muses and their hearts to be opened
1344 To infect and possess every being for which she had spoken
For she sensed the evil presence of the Demon
And knew that his vision of Los Angeles no one should believe in
She knew that this was not treason
For her father had succumbed to a devious spell
And did not know that the Demon wanted earth like hell
1350 Despite the goodness the Demon had hailed
The Son found the Sea in the heart of downtown
Where she was speaking to a crowd of the homeless bound
In opposition to the former nobility of the town
The Son sat and listened to her speak
With every word he watched the spirits around her get weak
1356 With every word the good in the city seemed to retreat

Here on this perch in Pershing Square I am here to preach
Not of peace or persecution but of demonology
Demons exist and they will possess your psychology
This city was never perfect it was just a simple illusion
So those minds manipulated and confused I want to reach
1362 I am not against good or its fusion
I just cannot let the city of my birth be deceived
By a demon who only wants to prove
That evil is willingly received
Now for those of you who question if evil is how I am moved
That maybe I am a demon, agony's muse, and here to dupe
1368 Let me ask those suspicious within my voice
Was goodness and purity your choice?
Or did the Sun waive his troubled hands and good became your law?
Free will is our only truth
And without an inquisitive call
Los Angeles was turned into this beacon of holiness
1374 You, nor I, none of the masses outside the fallacy of the church
Asked, we did not pray, for good and its boldness
This demon's task must be unearthed
The Sun shines bright, provides warmth and encourages growth
But it also creates deserts, it burns and fries
So the Sun being all good is all lies
1380 We cannot survive without the Sun, humanity needs light

But when the Sun sets and the Moon rises, light's hope
Is left to the Moon's dependence of the Sun's might
And that is not wrong until the Sun's advantage
Creates a desert of what was once fertile
The Sun's damage
1386 Can be insurmountable
So as you move around and across this space called Los Angeles
Remember that you own your free will
Do not let the guilt of being good be your thrill
Drugs made you feel better than you ever have
You were born to be dumb and reckless
1392 What you feel as bad
Could be to another good's fuel
And all that has been defined as good by the Sun
It has not been preferred by this earth's, this city's rules
Do not be fooled by what in good's name has been done

The Son approached the Sea after the crowd had dispersed
1398 For he understood her speech and its worth
And how Los Angeles by the Demon had been cursed
The Son knew the Demon and had once deceived him
So the Son knew that the Sea's whim
Was fatter than it was thin
The Son approached the Sea
1404 With honesty
That she could not flee

I know I may not deserve your attention
Are you a willing listener?
Wisdom knows your words and decisions
Wisdom knows deception and many fools but few practitioners
1410 I know that you are going to listen
Especially because what I have to say
Should be gospel, it will be, my novelty will be written
Then it will be studied and obeyed
I am pleased and honored that your ears are mine
Demons do exists and I have battled them perpetually
1416 Demons and this particular Demon have been my bane since time
And breath filled new lungs and minds knew good skeptically

Good has been demonized
And I come to you to understand your position
Is good coming from a Demon to be denied and scrutinized?
Or does evil define your intuition?
1422 The Sea is rocky and tumultuous
But it also controls commerce and feeds
So with the utmost respect I ask, what is your focus?
Do you want to move goods that benefit needs?
Or do you want those ships sunk?
Truly, I mean no disrespect for I am called the Desert
1428 And I understand the depression of goodness, its funk
But I also understand that goodness' intentions are not to hurt
I understand that this Demon has deceived this city
And your intentions are as beautiful as the sunset over the sea
But if your pity
Is only what evil may have done and what you perceive
1434 Is an anger that proves that you are mad at what was done
Because you could not do what was did
So your fun
Is to rid
The universe of this Demon that created good
In a space where you could not
1440 And never would
Because you are purely evil, and never possessed good's thoughts

Desert is how you identify?
Barren is your nature and those that survive your terrain are vultures
So for you to cast dispersion and swift judgment upon my culture
How do you know my natural inclinations?
1446 Is diverting accountability how I decide?
How can you judge or deem true my manifestation?
When your dryness only destroys life
You too must be under the spell of evil and its muses
For goodness seems to be your strife
Good was born in you and all it abuses
1452 But like me fatigue explains your descent
You have been maltreated by good and its supposed rewards
And you cannot help but expose evil not for what it affords
But because good has left you skeptical and mistrusting

So evil you expose so you can join its hoards ascent
Good is not Los Angeles or the universe that is rusting
1458 But you were once good and something changed
That is why you came to me the daughter of the Moon
Power and influence from you is not estranged
And for both you will not swoon
But to control this universe you must understand
That Father and the Moon and the Sun are corrupt
1464 And it is their influence we must disrupt
Demons have possessed this planet
They have ensured that goodness' plan
Must fail, Fatherdamn it!
That is not a goal I combat
If goodness is thrust upon the universe as how things should be
1470 Then I must retract
I am now against all things good because what was forced upon me
And your essence screams that same disposition
Good was forced upon you
And you tried to make do
But goodness and Father betrayed your perfection
1476 So your intuition
Only understood that good's fetish is evil's perception
The Desert is the Sun's greatest ally
For the Desert is the Sun's greatest creation
The Sun shines over the desert high in the sky
And the Sun is evil's grand elation

1482 You have still refused to answer my question
But I insist that I know the answer
Good has never been your predilection
It has always been your cancer
In that we are the same
And that is why I approached you today
1488 You are correct, I too want to see an end to the Demon's game
He is a prophet that was never sanctioned by heaven's gaze
Together we can thwart this fiend and his deceit
I want to challenge you not to let your longing for the Sun's doom
Punish Los Angeles we must remove the Muses of Agony's fleet
For they act on the Sun's behalf and must not loom

1494 Our collective will must endure longer
We must not allow our disdain for the Demon's earthly place
To overtake our hearts and minds while evil's muses get stronger
Their influence over the people we must forsake
And if you want Los Angeles to be yours
You must first rid the town
1500 Of all the muses and their hordes
Or it will be to their evil we are bound

We must stop the Muses of Agony?
You believe that we must fight for good?
And keep Los Angeles how the Sun would?
That is something I cannot suborn
1506 How in good conscience could we
Allow good as perceived by a Demon's swarm?
This great and wonderful city
I do not support or want what agony brings
But it would surely be a pity
If the Demon's battle cry we sing
1512 I will not fight the Muses of Agony
Not because I am against good and its uses
But because I am against the Sun and his abuses
The Muses of Agony were on their way here before the Sun
To save the fate of the city from them is not in me
If you alone are that savior then your will be done
1518 True interaction is needed in this city
To be maneuvered into good or evil is unnatural
It has been too easy to be your essence's antipathy
We should not be beholden to good because it is tactual

Evil is necessary that distinction I have made stubbornly
But to stand by and to allow evil to persist
1524 All stoic and ornery
Seems to me to be defeatist
You are not a creature of evil's behest
That I understand simply by our conversation
Thoughtful you are but you must confess
That good must confront evil's confrontation
1530 The free will of the Muses of Agony must not be appeased

        While your free will is focused on this Demon
        Who did more good than you pleased
        I admit his motives were to be mistrusted but good must be even
        You knew of this Demon and his motives
        Whilst her father believed the Demon to be a prophet true
1536   But to allow Los Angeles to fall to what evil supposes
        Is only giving the Demon his due
        He knew that you would despise his relationship with your father
        More than your disdain for his deeds
        The Sun knew you would not bother
        To try to truly defeat evil and its seeds

1542   The Sun was right to believe
        I will not try to fight the Muses
        I will only preach against the Sun's abuses
        Agony has only come to reclaim its territory
        Which it lost by how deceit feeds
        So when the Muses come to restore their glory
1548   And take Los Angeles like they had before
        I will be passive and accept their disputed path
        Despite what I abhor
        I want Los Angeles to be as I ask
        The city it was before the Demon's inception
        Before good's tyranny
1554   Before your infernal questions and their irritability
        Good and evil can and will exist here equally
        Without influence or condemnation or moral perception
        Good and evil can exist with contrary judgments equally
        And without the insinuation, dead
        That evil decisions we should always lament
1560   I realize my future actions will contradict all I have just said
        And to the Son of the Father and Father himself I will repent
        Fatherdamn it! The Muses must be stopped
        I am the only evil that this city needs
        So I will join your fight against evil's consuming greed
        I am not upholding the Demon's standards
1566   I just cannot allow for his props
        To continue to give this city answers
        This is my city to mold

Thank you for this realization
This is my city to mold
And you, Desert, will help with my evil and its facilitation

1572 The Desert and the Sea joined together to fight
The Agony that had begun to consume Los Angeles' light
For the city could not fall to evil's Muses and their might
San Francisco had just been purged
And evil and its insidious urge
Had been banned from the Bay Area but evil's scourge
1578 Still wanted Portland, Boise, Seattle and all of earth
But they would save Missoula, Dallas, and Fort Worth
Wichita, Kansas City, Houston, New Orleans, and Jackson's mirth
Saint Louis, Chicago, Cleveland, Minneapolis, and Nashville
Detroit, Indianapolis, Phoenix, Albuquerque, and Jacksonville
Philadelphia, Boston, Atlanta, New York City, Memphis will
1584 Be saved like the District of Colombia, Charlotte, and Miami
Guadalajara, Mexico City, Havana, and Calgary
Brussels, Rio de Janeiro, Toronto, and Buenos Aires
Due to the good of the Sun and the Moon's work
London, Cairo, Paris, Moscow, Jerusalem and Newark
Cape Town, Nairobi, Darfur, Rwanda, Islamabad, Beijing's worth
1590 Were decided by good because evil had been vanquished
Hong Kong, Tokyo, Minsk, and Dubai evil had relinquished
Sydney, New Delhi, had all been relieved by a good anxious
Baghdad and Amsterdam, Berlin, Istanbul, and Madrid
Kiev, Vienna, Kabul, Warsaw, and Prague denied what evil did
And almost from every city on earth evil had been rid
1596 The Sun and Moon accomplished their goal pure
From most cities on earth evil had been cured
Only two cities still had succumbed to an evil lured
They spent decades travelling
From city to city waging a war righteous and dazzling
But still they could not stop earth from completely unraveling
1602 Lagos proved difficult to save, good's lament
Terror, evil, and its possibilities reborn from the Dark Continent
Meant decades of fighting evil would have been in futility spent

I have gotten word from Los Angeles and it has fell

        Our task now is Lagos and to save these beautiful people
        Evil is sinister and only placed in disastrous hands
1608   But my daughter is my greatest worry so quickly we must dispel
        Evil from this city on the continent that birthed civilization's people
        Evil's problems in Africa have been the most difficult to stand
        Our greatest achievement has been freeing the cities here
        For the hurt and chaos that engulfed this land for centuries
        Has been absolved in most of this land
1614   Africa has experienced a hate more sincere
        Than Satan to Father or the prisoner to the penitentiary
        The abuse this land has taken for centuries should not stand
        But persistence is what oppression holds most dear
        And the oppression that I see
        Must have been sinisterly planned
1620   Although our mission is clear
        I cannot help but think about Los Angeles' grief
        It will not distract me from our mission on this land
        This journey has been arduous, rigorous, and troublesome
        Father's will is being done and earth is becoming what it should
        Evil's last breath is upon us so decades have not been lost
1626   But we must relieve Lagos and as soon as we are done
        We must rush to Los Angeles' aid, for if evil controls Hollywood
        All we have worked for will be lost

        Los Angeles being controlled by evil should be a concern
        And I understand how you yearn
        But that is not our current task
1632   We must focus on Lagos and how to rid evil from here
        A perfect planet is within our grasp
        Your daughter is from your loins so your heart she has
        If you have done anything against her spirit you must endure
        For evil's caste
        Will manifest in her
1638   She is your life so the city had been left with a caretaker fast
        To alleviate malevolence and keep evil away
        You must not let doubt sway
        The Muses of Agony are wickedness pure
        And only hearts indelible to what the rancorous say
        Should cause worry, torment, and misery

1644	Do not let the supposed fall of Los Angeles be a distraction made
	You know the plan the same plan we have employed
	That has managed earth into Father's favorable action played
	Your task is to destroy
	Destroy what the calamitous find potent, what they portray
	Evil cannot prosper unless hearts are open
1650	Have faith in the hands that hold your heart's token
	For you created that link
	Trust your daughter and that darkness will depart
	Do not let your confidence in her shrink
	Los Angeles will remained saved because of her heart
	Los Angeles is still the example for the universe, a beacon
1656	Evil will not rage
	Unless good has been weakened
	Los Angeles' demise has been staged

I attempt not to dwell on my city's fall
Honorable was our choice to protect Los Angeles
Faith is my guide to a lighter conscience
1662 And I understand further we cannot stall
We must save Lagos from maleficent flesh
My allegiance is to the people of Lagos, please remain confident
I just cannot help but wonder how Los Angeles could recede
After all the work we did to secure its salvation
All of our prayers, benevolence, and conviction are denied there
1668 So why wont any of the other cities and towns we relieved?
I believe that this is ordained and earth will be good's station
Forgive my doubt but I doubt only because I care

That is a valid question Moon, I understand why you are weary
So I will not chastise your inquiry
Truthfully, I do not know how any of those cities are protected
1674 We did our work and we told Father's truth
And our message was not ordained but elected
Our methods have not been uncouth
All we have done is preached the word to enrich hearts and minds
Hearts have been enriched and have also denounced agony
Minds have been empowered to fight evil's kind
1680 For those cities, for earth, and the universe I have sympathy

Remember that free will is humanity
And we cannot be consumed by the chaos of insanity
Father is our vessel and we have to trust Father as our guide
And if our trust relies upon the actions of the converted
Goodness must hide
But I believe that we have eliminated the truly perverted
We did not ask the citizens of earth to believe in Father's promise
We showed them good's vengeance
The citizens of earth understand that Death is most honest
Earth does not want to pay the price for evil's penance
Your question is valid still
It does not mean our global work succumbs to Los Angeles' will
This has already distracted us; we cannot let Lagos suffer further
We cannot dwell on what may happen
Now let us prepare to greet our sisters and brothers
They need our action

So the Sun and the Moon went about their task
And all that the Moon had asked
Would not last
The process of converting Lagos to pure good
Went on as it should
The Sun healed and the Moon preached what he could
But Lagos was not as gullible as other cities on the planet
They questioned Father's worth and care and were adamant
And knew that if Father was their salvation they were damaged
The people of Lagos, many questions they had asked
Especially questions about the Sun and Moon's task
And why Lagos was good's last task
The people asked about their free will and did they have a choice
Were they going to be relieved or subjugated by good's voice
Was the presence of good in their city to be rejoiced
The crowd began to get rowdy because they did not understand
Why the Sun and Moon felt the need to influence every human
To trust and know and believe in the will of Father as they planned
They being the two outsiders who travelled the globe
To purify the planet against evil and its hideous odes
Who refused to acknowledge that evil is also a choice chose
The Sun and Moon could not believe the upheaval

Although weary from their journey's struggle they were gleeful
Weariness would not defeat their message against an evil illegal
Despite the doubt of the people of Lagos the two remained strong
1722 For evil was and always will be wrong
Free will is no excuse for the ills that evil dawned
The more the Moon spoke and the miracles the Sun showed
Good seemed to be what Lagos supposed
And then willingly the demented would be exposed
Free will no longer included the right to be sinister
1728 Dispelled were the inclinations of the sinner
Most of the city would succumb to their gospel administered
But even still Lagos had a faction that refused their preaching
For they remember the history of Father's teachings
And how Father had used invaders to absolve murder and beatings
To rob the land of resources and riches, and to rape and pillage
1734 Their minds could not be moved to forget imperialism's image
Burned and bloody bodies littered demolished villages
No matter what good was professed by the Sun and the Moon
Broken families, poverty, global exploitation were untreatable wounds
Father could never relieve what was Lagos' ultimate doom
While the two captains of salvation attempted to sway
1740 The few in Lagos who denied good and its ways
Los Angeles was far from its better days
The Moon received a letter from a sender unknown
That requested that he rush home
For his daughter was trapped in a city with evil all alone
Although faced with their greatest test
1746 The Moon abandoned the Sun and Lagos' stress
The Sea was his only worry and her death would force regret
For the mission and all that he had endured for decades
An all good planet would be engulfed by shade
If he lost his daughter to evil's rage
The Sun knew that he would be abandoned
1752 For he understood the instinct of his weak companion
There was not another outcome the Sun could imagine
Lagos still had to be expunged of evil's dung
While the Sun worked on the mind's of those that questioned
And knew that what was being preached to them was dumb
The Moon was back in Los Angeles in search of his daughter

1758	As he traversed the city he observed the slaughtered
	Dismembered bodies and an enforced poverty fostered
	Despair and degradation on every street and block
	Main Street and Caesar Chavez the Moon would stalk
	Gage, Atlantic, Van Ness, Pacific, and Indiana he walked
	Soto, Slausen, Manchester, Bundy, Whittier, and Sunset
1764	From Imperial, Gardena, Redondo, and Santa Monica he fret
	He ran down Compton, Adams, Western, Crenshaw and wept
	The Sea could not be found on Abbott Kenney or Hollywood
	Westwood, Avalon, and none of their neighborhoods
	The Moon looked everywhere as long as he could
	He continued to search as days and weeks lapsed
1770	He searched until his body, like Los Angeles, had collapsed
	While on his knees the Moon heard a familiar voice relaxed
	Welcome home dad
	To the real Los Angeles, the one of free will
	Los Angeles before the Demon's will
	How do I know that the degradation you see is of the people?
1776	Muses of Agony attacked the city in great numbers sad
	And although I still preached from Father's steeple
	Goodness was denied by droves of those the Demon converted
	Survival was the mode and to ask for good against demand or need
	Is something that you subverted
	The people battled against good and its greed
1782	I witnessed the internal conflict and their struggle
	And did not easily decide against good
	That fact I willingly admit but good is not what most could
	Survival did not depend on good or evil but definition and need
	Most people are ignorant of what we juggle
	Their actions are not defined divinely or by hellish deeds
1788	The people need to eat and be housed and clothed
	And to preach that good will bring them all they use
	I cannot believe that that is what the Demon supposed
	Los Angeles is free of the Demon's perversion, his abuse
	The Moon lay stunned by his daughter's vitriol
	Fatigue set in as his mind had stalled
1794	And had no response for what the Sea installed

        Dumbstruck was the Moon
        For he knew his daughter had swooned
        Over a city doomed
        The Desert came and invoked
        Every insecurity the Moon spoke
1800   Hostility, the Desert provoked

        You do not recognize me Moon
        But certainly I know you
        Let me show you your familiarity, your doom
        You have been having dreams, true?
        About a life in heaven serving Father and the Son
1806   You fought the Demon your daughter abhors and you died
        Then waking from your bed became cumbersome
        Because you knew that your current life lied
        I am sure that Father finds you a supreme follower
        No matter the horrors you see, you still believe
        Blind faith is deceit's greatest borrower
1812   Life in heaven and here on a decrepit earth has been deceived
        In heaven your Father allowed a demon to seal your fate
        And that same Demon has been earth's salvation and freedom
        Belief in Father's perfection is fallacy because it has never been innate
        Not in all the universes and definitely not in the Sun
        The turmoil that you have experienced on this plane
1818   The Sun is its cause
        Is the world as you made it, to Father strange?
        Did Father come to you and ask you to enforce his laws?
        No, Father did not
        For I am Father's true son and you have been duped
        The Sun is a demon from hell hot
1824   The righteousness you think you know is a fluke
        Once you had wings and were my Father's greatest servant
        But your Father allowed this demon, your Sun, into heaven
        Now on earth, on bended knee, you are still fervent
        For the love of a Father who abandoned how you leavened
        All the riches of heaven, all the comfort that was ordained
1830   The family that you left behind in the midst of war
        Look at your strain!
        Where is your Father now that you bout with death once more?

1836
You are the Son of the Father?
I think, I believe that I heard you correctly
My intellect may be incapable of understanding what you said
But truly, you are the heir to the universe, the Son of the Father?
This is not a joke, if my daughter entertains you, I respectfully
Admit that I left Los Angeles in hands that are dead
You are the Son of the Father?
The second coming and the true salvation of the soul of humanity?
You? And you allowed Los Angeles to fall in this manner?

1842
Your claim compared to your actions is odd
Los Angeles has succumbed to the chaos of insanity
Glady, proudly, the Son of the Father watched evil raise its banner?
Admittance to such a preposterous notion only proves
Insanity is your definition
Look around you, this is the depravity Father's son suborns

1848
You call what the Sun accomplished a rouse?
But gore, apathy, and indifference are obviously your position
The arbiter of good in the entire universe, is now for evil forlorn
Witchcraft must be your profession, a sorcerer
Deceitful psychic that guessed my darkest thoughts and fears
My dreams are now being used for your abuses

1854
Look at this city and I should believe that you are its auteur?
The universe has been by your Father's will and design steered?
You must think that I am a fool and that my mind is useless
If you are not armed you are going to wish you were
For your blasphemy can no longer be endured
In the name of Father in heaven I condemn you to death

1860
Take up arms for Los Angeles will not succumb to your havoc
Let my blade cleanse your soul and rinse your lies
You have possessed my daughter you are a demon spawned
Now ends your reign in Los Angeles, tragic
You will not survive
You will not see the next day dawned

1866
Your will, will not match your accomplishment
Try, try, try, try, try, and mightily you will try
Seraphim your efforts has always garnered my admonishment
But by my hands you will die
Prepare for harsh and tortuous judgment

That will be impossible for you to survive

1872 The Desert and the Moon faced off in the streets of L.A.
The Sun was still in Lagos continuing the work they had made
For the earth he wanted to continue to sway
Lagos was still stubborn and good they refused
All the miracles that the Sun performed seemed a ruse
For the history of their land had been abused

1878 Lagos understood that outsiders had intentions selfish
And no more would they allow for invaders devilish
For they knew that outsiders cared not for their wellness
The Sun healed the sick and cured disease in the city
But still he did not garner some of the people's awe or empathy
And was eventually chased out of town by hate and enmity

1884 Lagos overwhelmingly decided against the input that had enslaved
Self-determination they craved
So a trip back to Los Angeles the Sun made
Lagos refused to be deceived again by outsiders
Good and evil and their subjection and its dividers
Were not to be determined by the will of liars

1890 Liars because the truth about the universe was not decided
By the people that the Sun and Moon had chided
Despite the path of righteousness guided
And all the earth and all its cities that had succumbed
Cities that had been made dumb
Because good was defined as a finite sum

1896 The Sun arrived and witnessed the destruction and devastation
Los Angeles had once been the beacon of elite human relation
The divisive factors that mired human complications
Had been eliminated and eradicated in earth and the universe
What was once a supreme example of the Father and his verse
Had become damned like the city had never relieved evil's curse

1902 In amazement the Sun walked the city
The Sun walked the same streets and blocks the Moon ran in pity
He approached the epic battle between the Desert and Moon civilly

Desert you must realize your disadvantage
Evil has always been as it will always be a coward's refuge
Your blasphemous claim makes you the greatest evil

1908	Each blow cast upon your damned spirit's vantage
	Has been absorbed like an abused helpless child's tears deluge
	Redeem your soul Desert if it is retrievable

I am the true Son of the Father and you are a peon
The wounds caused by your sword are tantamount to a paper cut
Take this blow and in the name of Death abscond
1914 Servitude is what you admire and desire in your gut
And you will realize that the Son of the Father is power
And the Sun you followed was a simple Demon and a farce
I am the Son of the Father and the Sun's influence and hours
Has proven that goodness is sparse
Once I kill you, you will go to heaven
1920 You have an undying belief in my idiot Father
And despite his current state, your goodness he will leaven
For he knows that its upkeep is no longer his bother
Take this other blow
Tell my father who sent you and that I am fine
He loves to know what he already knows
1926 Believe that this third blow will end your earthly time

Before the Desert struck that third and final blow
He was interrupted by the Sun who would show
That his motives the Moon, the Desert, nor the Sea knew or know

Seraphim before your fate is sealed by the Son of the Father
I would like to confess that I am your death's cause
1932 I am its cause now as I was its cause in heaven
Disbelief I am sure consumes you
For the physics of this realm has become your reverend
That is why awe was in your face when my miracles were due
Miracles were performed and you understood them as Father
Earth is not your home because of the Father or his will
1938 Heaven is your home because of me; I know that is a feeling odd
When I fell to earth my goal was to reinterpret Father's will
I wanted you to believe in goodness all over the earth
Your belief in true and genuine righteousness in the universe
Was my greatest tool

1944   Every miracle I preformed entranced and deceived your intrigue
       But still you are the greatest of fools
       Blindly you accept those who feign Father's reprieve
       That's when I knew that I felt sorry for you
       We saved most of the planet from the tyranny of hell
       But how can that be true
       When hell's author has heaven under his spell?

1950   Son of the Father lay that blow on the Seraphim's head
       And let him retreat to how he is led
       Then prepare to face the Demon who was cast
       Down to earth because of the Halo he placed
       Between the sharp horns on the Demon's chaotic head
       That Demon was I disgraced

1956   I must admit that the time I spent with you traversing the globe
       Helped me to understand that you are truly a good being
       Despite your penchant to be oblivious to my odes
       Fondness was not sparse in our travels, I hate seeing
       Your demise because of blade I do not wield or own
       But I have grown

1962   My dreams have been made true
       You are the Demon that haunts me
       The Son of the Father holds his sword above my head
       Let me receive what is due
       Allow my soul to flee
       For trust in a demon means my faith is dead

1968   The blow that the Son of the Father cast
       Ensured that the Seraphim's earthly life did not last
       The Son crass
       Made sure that the Demon witnessed his wrath
       In the Seraphim's death the Demon did not bask
       Despite a pitiful affinity for the Moon the Sun had grabbed

1974   Desert as you call yourself you will regret
       Sending the Moon back to the Heaven you fret
       How can you forsake your Father?
       Did he do you like he had done Satan and me?

            The Father professed good and goodness bothered
            An ungrateful Son could never see
1980   The chaotic nature of the universe he is heir
            How can you rule a universe that you do not understand?
            Disorder, chaotic nature, and discord is fair
            Omnipotence cannot describe or inform omniscience's stance
            Travelling the world with the Seraphim helped me know
            That subservience was his greatest foe
1986   The Moon served and honored Father without question or division
            Not because he was dumb or a fool
            But because he believed and had deathless faith in Father's vision
            He will be your Father's greatest tool
            Against your disobedience and in propagating a faith undying
            Now let me take up arms against the Moon's setter
1992   Watch as the Sun rises to destroy darkness for a time vying
            To be better

            The Son and the Demon took up arms as the Sea watched
            She watched timidly but guarded as she awaited her spot
            The Sea knew that only by her instincts she was taught
            Once again the Seraphim stood in heaven, a heaven unrecognized
1998   Rivers and lakes were either engulfed in flames or dried
            The atmosphere was now consumed with pride
            Mansions and gold roads had been pillaged
            Heaven had become an impoverished and decrepit village
            Filled with the ill souls who deny good's resilience
            The Seraphim walked heaven like those Los Angeles streets
2004   Trying to discover what had happened to purity and its feats
            Dumbfounded, tears trickled down both his cheeks
            The first prison in heaven the Seraphim encountered
            After sending the guards to earth floundered
            The Father's cell he approached timidly like a doubter

            Father is that you locked up like a criminal, a fiend?
2010   You will soon be free for the universe needs your guidance
            Satan owns heaven, how can that be accepted?
            Omnipotence cannot be caged or unseen
            The universe is upon you reliant
            So Satan, the Demon, and even your Son must all be rejected!

Seraphim you are loyal to me and that I honor
But as the Father I cannot forsake my Son's bother
Just like in your heart you know that your daughter's dissent
Is something that you must reinvent
Thank you for my freedom
I knew that you would not succumb to treason
Or earth and its deceitful pleasures
Please understand that your heart I wanted to measure
Satan was once as devoted as you
And despite my omniscience, free will does what it do

With my free will my lord I released you from this prison
Heaven is yours to own
So let us defeat this savage and reclaim your realm
The universe must know that good has risen
Evil spells, degradation, malevolence, and hate must be disowned
Father let me help you retake heaven's helm

I will follow you from out this cell and then out this prison
And recreate the heaven in my visions
But I must witness for myself the destruction and strife
And witness my heaven under the umbrella of night
Despite the stigma of demonology I have noticed from my cell
That when light absconds and darkness drops its veil
Satan and his Muses of Agony actually sleep
Satan does not care for the universe or its sheep
He also finds solace and relief in fulfilling his dreams
So for the universe he no longer schemes
If Satan cared about furthering his cause
There would be strict changes in universal and celestial laws
Good would die on earth and never drink from heaven's well
But they would rot in an empty, barren, and leaderless hell
The Demon was brought here once to prevent hell's ascension
An unraveling universe was not my intention
But I cannot help but witness how chaos influences the soul
Free will I gave to everyone but the angels so the legend is told
Good is more attractive than evil and being foul
So free will is not essential to what they vow

Look around and see how heaven looks like a city ungoverned
2052 Los Angeles' mystical destructive lore is in this heaven learned
I should have never allowed this to happen here
This is the free will I have feared

Heaven was still
The Seraphim and Father walked and observed against their will
An unrecognizable paradise evil filled
2058 Father seemed to never truly understand free will or its vices
For Satan never slept for he knew Father's message would entice
A savior to try to regain the universe that evil sliced
Satan was not omniscient or omnipotent but he was diligent
Rest was something not scheduled or relevant
Intelligence was not sparse and Satan's time was spent
2064 In observation of blueprints and strategy of a new a war
Heaven would always be fought for
For evil is chaos and stability is what most implore
Satan's vision for heaven was clear
Free will he wanted Father to fear
Satan addressed his will in his mirror

2070 Father is free, as I knew he would be
All knowing? Omniscience must be a myth
How could father not understand that arrogance is earned
My moves are not chaotic
Self-awareness and actualization are important in a new leader
And in myself I have found pride and indifference
2076 Pride that believed that once I conquered heaven I had won
Indifference that did not conceive of a father free from prison
An indifference that did not care who came or left here
But that is not how I operate now
The universe is fragile and if I want to control how it breaks
And how it cracks I better become more attentive
2082 How can my arrogance disregard father's power?
My arrogance allowed for father to once again patrol heaven
And fight for the thrown that I now sit
I now own my arrogance
For an eternity I have held my guard
I refused to find ease in battles against good and its utility

2088　Heaven I will not relinquish easily
　　　　Father and the seraphim will continue to hear silence
　　　　They can absorb the grim landscape that makes me comfortable
　　　　As the Muses of Agony and my armies prepare for the greatest war
　　　　That universe has ever known
　　　　I have ruled hell for eons
2094　My tyranny ensured that all of the cell's in every chamber
　　　　Were filled, over crowded with suffering and regret
　　　　The entire universe will be filled the same with beings who know
　　　　Only the subjugation I force into their hearts
　　　　I will not move on the seraphim or father yet
　　　　Until I prepare all my hoards on all planes of existence
2100　Humans versus demons versus angels versus gods
　　　　The universe will be by my design charged
　　　　Or it will implode

　　　　Father it is eerily quiet here
　　　　But I trust in you and will not hide
　　　　I walk beside the auteur of the universe openly in paradise
2106　I will not question our path or quiver in fear
　　　　For I feel safe by your side
　　　　By your side is where I will stand in this new war devised

　　　　War is once again imminent my son
　　　　For my will it will be done
　　　　I will no longer allow for free will to determine destiny
2112　How could I allow for my Son to decay to my enemy?
　　　　Seraphim we must find those who are still good here
　　　　I know there is an underground revolutionary network geared
　　　　To ensuring that war comes again
　　　　If we lose this time enmity may force the universe to re-begin

　　　　If angels that did not fall to the Muses of Agony are still here
2118　I will find them and gather them for revolutionary action is near
　　　　We will be Satan's fear
　　　　To all of your wishes I adhere
　　　　The triumphant cheers of the good and all the choirs I can hear
　　　　Because evil in all the universe soon will have disappeared

           After a ten-year battle the Demon's earthly form lay lifeless
2124   In the middle of a Los Angeles in midst of an identity crisis
           The news carried the battle so did all national network devices
           Battles between the Desert and the Sun were made into movies
           Music from all genres were influenced by the conflict's beauty
           The passionate battle influenced plays, paintings, novels and poetry
           Devoted to the growth and prosperity of the city of Los Angeles
2130   The citizens of the city including the Sea understood the jealous
           They knew that this battle between two pious zealots
           Has created commerce that revitalized the city
           The epic battle fell into the background and life was restored newly
           And Los Angeles became what it was before the Demon's plea
           The Desert and the Sea could begin their reign
2136   Before their decree could be claimed
           The Sea addressed the Demon nearly slain

           And that Demon ends your deceitful regime
           No more will earth succumb to your crooked intentions
           No more will we be exploited by your hideous invention
           I knew my intuition was strong
2142   I knew that your belief in good was a dastardly scheme
           I knew in my head and heart that it was for evil you longed
           Los Angeles is whole and soon earth will be once more
           There are not sides to be chosen, one side is not more true
           Humanity in singular moments decides what to implore
           Evil shall remain here, good too, but not you

2148   The Demon paralyzed only had a few breaths to breathe
           And with each one he squeezed
           The Sea's heart he attempted to seize
           Before he passed on into hell
           The place he found most swell
           Where a new leader and evil would swell

2154   I have always understood you Sea
           Even more than you have thought to understand me
           You knew I was inherently evil in my heart and soul
           But what evil did I perform?

What was my will's toll?
You make me most happy because good is not a reform
2160 I never displayed or admonished openly sin
I tried to disavowal humanity's fall and return earth to the day
Before sin in their DNA was written
But Sea you proved that evil is growth not decay
The good I vetted around the globe
Was the antithesis of your ode
2166 You had no evidence to my evil past
And you judged me to the point of committing evil acts
And that evil in you will persist more than the good will last
It was always good that you lacked
What you described as intuition
Is how the fool attributes his foolishness to ignorance
2172 Evil is your predilection
Soon the Desert will become your adversary not your deference
Home sweet home
Eternal warmth, closure for a lifetime of malevolence grown
I see the souls damned because they made mistakes
Souls that need leadership to define their roles
2178 But in this new hell I will raise the stakes
I need a well trained, intelligent, and a strong army to impose
The will of true evil in all of the universe
No longer will I accept the Muses of Agony
The Honest Honorable are now the Damnable cursed
With the task of rivaling those Muses tragically
2184 Satan has proven that evil is not his prime motive
His actions only jealousy exposes
Earth understood that good is subjective especially in Father's name
All of earth almost fell to goodness
Lagos and the Sea proved to shame
That Father's purity was complete fallacy and ruthless
2190 A neglected hell is now my throne
All of its depths and its chambers its influence will be renewed
For this hell I will roam
For the most intelligent and brilliant minds misused and abused

the poems
(2013-2016)

"there is only one corner of the universe you can be certain of improving and that's your own self." – aldous huxley

the sun

Not for nothing is your life's pride
And its path, your dad won't decide
They won't either
Her? Him? Definitely not her or him or their believers
Always be sure and never hide
Never run lest to the sun's fever

Ignorance is all life is
Embrace the task of discovering this
Life is not what daddy thinks
Journey and find that when life kinks
Arrogantly, decide that it won't subsist
Constant is one who knows their instinct

Omniscient I don't ever want to be
But I will surely try, you'll see
Son you'll grow weary of me and my thoughts
Hell, you may rebel against all I've taught
Ensuring that the greatest gift you'll ever get from me
Probably, is questioning everything ever sought

Pursue who and what your heart will know
And understand that your father only hopes to show
Real love and dedication and their fallacy
Don't choose to disagree
Can you know me like I hope you grow?
And know that my heart is all you'll be?

So, pardon all of my insecurities son
To be? Is only to be recognized and will only be won
Even if you have lost
Let me know how much it cost
Life is something that breath cannot buy or numb
Adventure my son, is willingly enduring chaos

Nathaniel please try to understand your dad and his flaws
Ouch means that I've burnt your paws
Singed is the soul I never had
Maybe it is your light that has driven my darkness mad
Your life has illuminated my lurid laws,
So don't ignore my fury or its corruption and its fad

Oh, my beautiful and brilliant baby boy for you I will do anything
Night, night to the dusk. Thank you Nathaniel Jacob Sheppard for being

the trees that live forever

The forest is gone
That is only sad if trees
Do not become books

save the newspapers

I may be a little late
But this is a rallying call
Free speech's vitality, its fate
Is slipping into biased hands
Hands that could only rape
And destroy free thought
This is not my biased take
Just watch local and cable news
Listen to news radio ache
And bemoan any sense of objectivity
Journalists must not break
We must fight with them
And support what they make
The news at an angle
An angle that isn't bought or shaped…
Well…
Hopefully it hasn't been…
Actually, save the trees!

beach day

I checked the weather report the night before
Tomorrow it's going to be 91 degrees in Boyle Heights
The beaches are going to be in the low 80s
"Babe, tomorrow is a perfect beach day"
We woke up excited, ready to hit the sand and the shore
Ready for the sun and its ambivalence
I pack my bag like every beach day
Something to drink, something to read and something to smoke
Swim trunks and a towel, also an old blanket
My lover packs sunglasses, a two-piece, and sunscreen
We take the 704 Santa Monica Rapid Bus
Three hours later we arrive at Santa Monica beach
We both have to piss like crazy
The traffic on the Westside is abhorrent and interminable
We rush to the bathroom, we piss then we hit the sand
I take off my shoes, she takes off her sandals
All four feet hit the sand then we walk towards the ocean
We lay down the old blanket as best we can
The wind likes to interfere with perfect placement
I use my towel to let her change into her two-piece
The same towel covers me into my swim trunks
She then lays on her stomach studying Physiology or something
I use her butt as a pillow, reading The Corner or something
She opens her drink then I open mine, we make a toast
A toast to beach days and the sun and the ocean air
A toast to us and how we got here and making our way back home

it rained last night

It rained last night
As I left my apartment this morning
The ground was wet and the concrete had grown moss and mold
The hard rain had chipped the paint of all the cars
A stray dog was drinking from a puddle
While a tsunami of birds circled
Waiting for their chance to take a drink
Of the paint and oil soiled reason for life
It rained last night
The people I passed all had umbrellas and rain coats
Anticipating a rain that had already passed
Like all of the cars splashing puddles onto the sidewalk
An old man and his grocery bags were buried
He raised his cane like a rifle with no ammunition
Shooting his stare like a fully automatic at the car
Already three blocks away
It rained last night
The air feels fresher than it usually does
You can breathe easier and deeper
And you won't cough up your lungs or puke your stomach
The dewdrops on the desert flowers are mirrors
That the hummingbirds and butterflies and beetles
Use to deny their ignorant vanity
Because they know that they will die if they take a peek or a drink
It is raining
So I run back to my bed
Tap! Tap! Tap! Tap! Tap! Cease-less tapping
On my window and roof as I try to dream
Tap! Tap! Tap! Laying in my bed thinking of tap-dancers and their annoying shoes
And hideous monster rain drops drowning my heart
Thinking of a flood of birds staring at me then drinking my flesh
It is raining Tap! Tap! Tap!
I cover my head to keep from getting wet; the water is at my waist

nature

Majestic mountains in the bold background
Frame a lovely lake surrounded by titanic trees
The sun is shimmering on the lake's wonderful waves
The path we patrol cuts clear across a magnificent meadow
Fabulous flowers pray at our soulful soles
Inhaling has never been this incontrollable or easy
Hawks are hollering and hovering over malnourished mice
A deer is drinking water from a surprising spring
Before running away to chase a fine fawn
A scene salaciously serene
Novel, necessarily nutritious, and nice nature
Beauty and all of its bounty bare to our eyes
But we cannot stay still, we must move from here
Soon the trees will be tumultuously cut and cleared
The mountains morosely will shade a small town
And line and comprise the luminous roads ridden down
The town swims in the polluted lake placed next to the depleted spring
All those drinks celebrate the deer that screams as they sing
The fearful fawn watches her husband as he is enjoyed and eaten
The hawks hover over rooftops looking and listening for rats speakin'
Flowers will be feverishly plucked to protect feelings wavering
Willows fall from the deathly windows and die enabling
Decomposing on the slate sidewalks all but the mountains disremembered
A setting exceptional in soliciting an erased nature disfigured
I wish I were born in nature's bounty
Organically grown only needing what I knew cunning
Secure and sheltered by her care undoubting
I wish that delicious deer had kept running

dead broke

Nothing
No coins
No credit cards
No assets
No money
Nothing to offer
And nothing to sell
No one will pay to fuck me
No job
Dead broke
Potatoes for breakfast
Potatoes for lunch
And potatoes for dinner
Potatoes for dessert
Faucet water
Hand washed laundry
Jump the turnstile for the train
To go nowhere
Here comes the Metro police
And here comes the train
There I go
No coins
No credit cards
No assets
No money
No life
Dead broke

heavy lifting

I am a heavy guy
I'm 6'3" and about 240 pounds
That's a lot of weight to carry around
I don't carry all of it though
I think I lug about 115 pounds around town
The other 125 pounds others carry
My girlfriend carried the bulk of the errant 125
She carries about 70 pounds
My brother carries about 30 pounds
My friends 10
And my grandparents the remaining 15
It's a lot of weight for them to hoist on their backs
Especially considering that they must carry their own
Recently, my girlfriend threw those 70 pounds back onto my shoulders
It is really heavy
I'm up to a cool 185 now
And it's weighing me down
But it's also making me stronger
When I get strong enough I'm going to ask my brother for my pounds
And then I'm going to ask my friends and my grandparents to return my fat
And then I'm going to bend my knees and lift with my legs
And carry all that weighs them down

the nihilist who cares

I do not care now
About you, not anything true
Expressed by my tears

numb

I have never felt
At least that's what I tell myself
My heart is broken I think
But I did not feel it shatter or its pieces sink
I have never felt and I do not feel
Happiness I think is real
I know how to mimic people who say
That happy is how they feel today
But it is numb
It is not genuine, it is dumb

starving

Information is
All around us, waiting too
To be devoured

low-life

I am not going to amount to much
That's what she told me
My dreams are a waste, they're too tough
My ambition is weak
I was told that I am a low-life
Society's most dreadful and bleak
A magnet for ridicule and spite
"You will be nothing, no one to seek
And you will miss and regret not having me around"
Maybe I am nothing
And maybe I am a low-life hound
A person of poor character and of nothing
Someone who deserves humiliation and antipathy
But what I know for sure
Is that I won't succumb to apathy
It has to matter what I have endured
This barrage of judgment about my life
A life that I am still living
A low-life, a scoundrel that no one will ever love, you are right
I am all you said, unforgiving
You were only wrong about one risk
I am going to "miss and regret" not having you around, you say?
I only regret that you exist

you are wrong

You know how to reach as many people as possible?
Say something, anything, just say it simply
You can get a population to agree, a population docile
Will agree to anything as long as it is empty
It does not have to mean anything truly
"I started from the bottom and now I am here"
Unsure if I can see my destination clear
I just know that the bottom cannot fool me
No new friends will I gain here either
My success is only stringent upon my own will
I did it by myself, I was the only feature
How happy I am to know still
That all that helped me was this one song
That told me that everyone else around me
Was wrong
And my selfish thoughts were all that were necessary
Although the bottom has not been defined
And neither has now, right here
For agreement amongst most billionaires refined
Define your worth, as worthy as you are, as the bottom

shot-put

The weight of the world
Is on my shoulders heavy
Throw it or be crushed

los angeles

I am not from here
But I am
I can't help but recognize how different I am
I also can't help how I am the same
I love it here
I love the smell and the people
The other transplants who denigrate this city's worth
I love them because they make me feel better
This beautiful city in the heart of old Mexico
This city undefined, vast in its indifference
I love Los Angeles
There is nowhere else that means anywhere
I love Los Angeles
And if you don't
Let us walk you to the border gleefully
For if you don't love it here
You hate yourself

yesterday's waste

Morning, wide-awake
Lying in bed decaying
Bathroom a-waiting

scented commute

Another dreary morning my alarm clock admits
Still weary from the hours I can't rest
I rise from my bed and walk into a pot of coffee
The day I dread while my coffee brews
A piss, a shave, a shower
Black jeans or grey? To black I cave
My shirt the same color as the back of my eyelids
Still dreaming that I don't have to work

Three or four blocks away is Soto Station
My destinations golden first path
It smells of tamales, champurrado
Elote, and pan dulce as my stomach wails
The ride is smooth, viejitos and students
Nurses and the homeless man with a stench crude
The tamalera's treats being eaten from the train's seats
Overpower the smell of the homeless man's feet

I transfer to Union Station
Los Angeles' congested hub, my trips next answer
My face flushed red from the smell of perfume and cologne
All of the cups of coffee cannot displace
The smell of everyone who can only smell better than they look
The people are tired from being tired and never understand
How their perfume's pleasantry is not for all noses
Luckily my stop comes soon

Another train at 7th and Metro Station
My face joins the others who can't act, our faces blue
For we're being carried further and further away from our beds
The air is stale, no smell worth seeing
I don't think my nose could ever tell
There is not a smell that it can discern, that it knows
When the projects are on both sides of the tracks
I realize that my ride is closer to work than home

The Willowbrook station means I'll be working soon
We ride alongside the the freeway, jammed with green cars
How they wish that they could move as swiftly as us
On this train I smell optimism about the day
Sleep isn't all I should want or know
I am conscious and prepared for everything that would
Finally, I arrive to work. Those hours I didn't sleep forgotten
Hopefully, I'll be awake for the rest of this dreadful week

charade

That mask masquerades
As your frightened face, hidden
I like how you look

sleep training

On this desolate platform
A man rests on a bench
Asleep from the day's malaise
He is unaware of the breeze in the tunnel
That warns that the train is approaching
I stand here waiting alone
The train's lights get closer and closer
As the breeze gets stronger and stronger
It was an oddly chilly night
Especially for the first day of summer
My jacket blew in the trains fabricated wind
The trains lights blind as it arrives
Distorting the conductor as I shield my eyes
I board the empty car
Guided by the ghost conductor
And stand until I reach my stop
I walk the vacant streets home to rest
My bed's debility keeps my mind full
Wondering what is more comfortable
My bed or that man's bench

corrido

This is a story about a gangster who runs
He runs guns
Drugs and liquor and cigarettes
And women
Coke up his nose
Heroin in his veins
His flask full and then emptied
Cigarette after nervous cigarette
Running up the west coast of México
From Jalisco through Nayarit
His paranoia worsens as he runs through Sinaloa
All the way to the US Border at Sonora
How his goods reach the Los Angeles streets
No one knows
But with every run his paranoia still shows
Very abusive is this gangster
He runs with his habits
But of his women he never partakes
Abusive towards their beauty
And its temptation
It's distracting to his work
Women he knows are the most dangerous of all
For this gangster knew of love only once
A beauty from Guadalajara
Long jet-black hair
Skin soft and golden
He loved her so and will never love another
For she was once his only addiction
One that he is still grieving
When she ran away
Only his mirror knew of his tears
He hates his women most of all
Possessors of beauty that any man would swoon
For he knows that any affair
Any lingering feeling at all
Will soon be a distant reflection
So he keeps running

spurious

Curious, I am
I trusted that you were real
You are a knock-off

sobriety and its horrors

I just finished my drink
And it is going to be my last one for a while
I think
No more will I vomit bile
Because the night before
I couldn't handle all that I had to drink
No more beer, wine, or liquor
So unclouded I should think
Now my vision is clearer
No longer is my progress impeded by a substance
That causes my true judgement to disappear
I am free of pollutants substantive
I am honest with who I see in the mirror
My abstinent mind is steady and level
And I still am a devil

need

Your love is all I'll ever need
It is how I feed
Forgive my hate and me
But your love is my fate
I've tried my love, to let you go
Many times you know
But your love is too strong
It always holds on
You knew that when years passed
That you'd only want me alas
What always confused me most
Is what you soon will boast
My ignorance, you'll decree
Did not know that we'll always be
Something that you always knew
Is that my hate would always be few
I love you with all of my heart
Just remember this poem's start

a perception nonetheless

The fool gets credit
For having some discernment
Foolish is the fool

dead forest

Suddenly, you're in a forest
Surrounded by Firs and Pines
The bottom of the sky
Is the top of the trees
You hear barking and buzzing
Crows and growls and chirping
The midday fog is thick
The sun only seems to lengthen shadows
And you can't see the dogs or the bees
The foxes or the birds
You feel your way through the mist
Until you can't feel anymore
The sun is beginning to set
You were feeling around that forest for hours
Snakes underneath your feet
A river of a stream had soaked your boots
You look up at the sky to see the time of day
The sun is setting over the barren hills
The orange glow of the sun reflects
The neon orange of safety vests and yellow of hard hats
You are barely taller than the big rubber tires
That destroyed centuries of nature's building
In only eight hours
Now the sun has set
And you must return home
You proceed as you had come
The moon is full and high
Brightening the owl on the branch
The deer looking for a nice place to sleep
As the rodents squeak through your feet
You scurry to the foot of your bed
To pray for that forest dead

the nicest buildings in the neighborhood

The worth of a neighborhood is determined by its architecture
Not the style, although it is true
That the style you choose or embrace could determine your stature
What I rue
Is that certain institutions are worth more than others
It makes sense I suppose
Those institutions, our economic growth they smother
Now what institutions are those?

The police station is one of grand merit
The most oppressive physically
Not even darkened streetlights could forget
The assault on bodies and minds and the local economy
Prisons pay Hollenbeck Station well
A new barn with new troughs
They hope every untaxed business fails
So that their home is modern and nice how it ought

There is a beautiful hospital near my home
Doctors and nurses and other health professionals can help
Our community is riddled by disease and is violence prone
A new, larger emergency room and a bigger staff tell
That this hospital will be busy forever
How beautiful are the buildings that house
Bodies victimized by a neighborhood clever
A neighborhood whose pain can't be espoused

The funeral parlor down the street is well structured
Bodies battered and bruised, hard workers of industries
That the police and the county and the state rupture
Limos and low riders, classics and modern imports
Are a moat around a beautiful building of celebration
Celebrating lives in peril and those of innocence and calm
Lives thought to survive the hospital and those whose time had been
Tall Roman columns laud mothers with their faces in their palms

Those bodies at the funeral parlor are destined for a church
Where absolution and explanation for death will come
Before those sons and daughters are hauled off to the cemetery's dirt
The pastor or the priest will measure a life's sum
A Spanish Gothic building filled with woodgrain pews
The stained glass windows enlighten confessionals
Every sin that is spewed
Is a dollar towards the lifestyle of a church and its religious professionals

The grocery store sells frozen meat and nearly expired vegetables
One of the worst high schools in the city still graduates our future
Community centers and parks are poorly maintained and unsuitable
But as long as our lives can be impeded by those creatures
Who only use our bodies to make a living
We will always live in pest-infested apartments
Government housing will always be perceived as giving
And our lives we will forever lament

one leg

Hop, hop, hop, hop, hop
Hop, hop, hop, hop, hop, hop, hop
Hop, hop, hop, hop, hop

conformity factory

Out of this machine comes another
Another person who will listen
Someone who will be told what to wear
In this model imprisoned
For all of their care
Will reside in the other

You see what they say
You watch what they listen to
Then you mirror
A copy of a copy of a copy is you
Popular opinion tells you much clearer
Than the brightness of day

It is okay to like what is most sought
I understand that it's all about connection
And some reach others better
Marketing geniuses whose election
Is suspect and mysterious and tethered
To what impressionable idiots wrought

Feign complexity and intellect
Only to retard substance and depth
Use symbols and terms easily accessible
Use minds simple and adept
At relaying how contrarian thought is detestable
"Differing opinions you must neglect"

Conform you do
To all that you're told
Watch this film and listen to this album
To you only these clothes are sold
Off of the assembly line you come
Adopting all forced into your purview

aplomb

They are distracting but keep calm
Imperturbable you are
You must continue even if you are wrong
Your composure can't be marred
In most situations you tend to believe
That anger or anxiety is flawed
So you steady your hands and knees
And deny those thoughts impossible to laud
For worry and uncertainty you cannot appease
Despite how much they tease
They can't, they won't get to you
Their novelty isn't true
Focus on the task at hand
And continue on your path as planned

the time of the bastard iconoclast

This is the age of the iconoclast
There is no definition
And if there is, its been dissolved
It isn't the glory of the inverted cross
Or the re-appropriation of the swastika
It isn't Odin's rune or the ankh
Those who were dead live anew
Words Tupac Shakur never said bare his name
And movements he would be against
He sponsors

Marilyn Monroe's spirit is defeated
By her worship
Those who attempt to honor her life
Only denigrate what her sexuality did
For a country prude
Mickey Mouse as a heretic
Chanel's quality disfigured
Great philosophers and poets create what they hadn't
Prominent figures whose art is abandoned
For popular culture's carnage

Images and symbols are being destroyed
Only to be rebuilt to engage strange dialogue
For capitalist gains and repetition
What was represented is denied
There are no venerable symbols
All are conquered by a new rhetoric
One that excuses ignorance and misinformation
I don't believe in definition
But I also know that this is invalidating
How do you mold who someone was?

Why deny why a symbol was created?
Why doesn't your vision acknowledge
How they were defined?
Or how they defined themselves?
What in them told you
That Tupac would accept your vision?

That Ms. Monroe would honor your collection?
Would Chanel honor your caliber?
Does Plato or Shakespeare know you?
Do you know them?

There is a lull in creation
That must change what was made
Because individuality is owned
And instead of inspiring
It is trending to mimic
There is no nobility in this destruction
No solace can be taken in reviving
Spirits who only want rest
As this age progresses
Old art is demolished by laziness

This time will be forgotten
And the negatives of the images stolen
Will live as they once did
And the generations after us
Will create new definitions and new art
From emotions and thoughts that seem archaic
They won't try to change the past
They will deny this faux revolution
And not forgive these bastards
For their dishonor

why are they laughing?

Excited you are
Go ahead, I deserve it
Stop laughing, will you?

beauty mask

Oh, how beautiful you are
Every blemish and every scar
Your high cheekbones and even jaw
Define a face pretty and raw
But since your birth you were told
To hide your face and fold
You must distort and achieve
A deception that magazines appease
Men always say
"How pretty you look today"
Your legs long and exposed
The lovely pattern on your toes
The slit in the back of your skirt
Leads to the most heavenly place on earth
And how most men seem to get there
Is acknowledging that mask that frames your stare
Those chemicals that eat your skin
Govern the confidence behind your grin
Bright red lipstick lay the foundation
Eyeliner, mascara and their patience
Deal with a barrage of compliments scorned
Until the right one from the right man is sojourned
You take him home and to your sheets
He gives you what you both had to seek
In the morning when you wake
The pillow wears your second face
And when he looks you in your nude eyes
Past last night's visual lie
He goes away
And another man refused to stay
This mask you wear so pretty that all the outside sees
Ignores the cries of the beauty underneath

black coffee

One more cup of coffee
I don't remember how many I've had
A typical morning
To get through this day without yawning
I need coffee to last
So I won't get… I can't get… sleepy
Another cup down the hatch
I am still writing, work must be done
I won't be sleeping anytime soon
A couple more cups a little past noon
Jittery me, sitting here writing for fun
Breaking only to ground beans for my coffee, black
Into the night I write, as if it were day
Awaiting another sleepless morning's fray

equality? impossibly!

Everything will be
Equal when capitalism
Does not exist here

my opinion sucks

On that subject
I have a lot to say
Listen to my objections
Listen to my dismay
You must be crazy
To think that way

fiction

There's nothing like telling the truth
It isn't as hard as people make it seem
It can be endured and has been
Facts are great barriers to imagination
But a real world is seeking real answers
And lies tell stories impossible to perceive
Decidedly, obscuring reality's mission

"The dragon is the murderer!" I was once told
"I could not have committed those crimes
I was with the pixie at the time
What time was that you ask?
It was the time the ocean sank
We both had to walk the plank
So ask the pirates, they'll tell you

That dagger in evidence isn't mine!
Neither could the pixie's wand have been used
Because by our own weapons we were subdued
The threat of the dagger's blade sent me into the ocean
As did the wand to the pixie, scared
Challenge the pirates we would never dare
The dragon is the murderer, believe me!

Dragons breathe fire
And the victim was charred
Dragons have sharp teeth, large
Although the same size as my blade
My dagger was in my back
And not murdering some poor sap
It was the dragon I tell you, the dragon

Please, leave the pixie alone
Dragons can also fly
And I've already given you our alibi
So the long fall that the victim took
Only to crash in the middle of that meadow
Had to take strength, you know?
So leave the pixie's wings alone!"

That's what he told me
This morbid villain told me that a dragon had done it
This child was stabbed 28 times and then set on fire
We found his dagger drenched in their blood
That meadow underneath a cliff
Was not a meadow but the bottom of a canyon
Found by a couple hiking
His story was true, he'd insist
I wish pixies and dragons did exist
For some horrors should only be of imagination
And not simply experience and its replication
Haunted forever by this victim
How I wish some monsters were fiction

a writer's memory

Writer's memory
Only tells the truth sometimes
When convenient to

dead i am: i'm joining the club

I'm joining the club
My life is over
Dead I am
Breath still in my lungs
Breathing constantly and indomitably
But dead
Like Janis Joplin
Like Kurt Cobain
Like Jimi and his riffs
I am dead
I didn't think I'd live this long
I just knew I'd be dead by at least 25
Like Tupac Shakur
When that year passed alive
I thought I'd die at 26
Just like Otis Redding
But here I am, dead at 27
Club 27 I join
Amy Winehouse is here
So are Jim Morrison and Basquiat
Dead I am
Misunderstanding is wherever I've been
Unknowingly drifting into a life forged anew
To breed life
And all of its fallacy
Wishing that I created a standard
Envious of the envy the others in the club created
My life is over
Alive I hoped to be for longer
But dead I am
The life that will be lived
Is growing
He won't falter
He will be me alive
I'm joining the club
The world will appreciate my art
The universe will understand

That my rebirth
My heart
Is my son, smart

simulacrum

I know who you are
Your words and thoughts are not new
A copy, copied

the moral monster

For this reason we must act
Morals are all that must be recognized
Subjectivity and its belief is ignorance
There is no morality outside of my guise
Now this is all that can only make sense
This is decency and its map
I solely reckon with help
These deeds favorable to be acknowledged
By the unrighteous dissenters
Those who deny morality's pledge
Must obey what your wickedness splinters
Bow coyly to morality's wealth
If you refuse my objection
Your body, your mind, and soul's use
Will face abuse in the absolute name
Of the cause of your abuse
Why suffer your immoral pain?
Why live in the manner of my rejection?
Insane you are to deny my persuasion!
To deny morality, indiscriminate and appropriate
I will force you to know your error
I attempted to warn you and your associates
Now you must all adhere to my furor!
Pain, agony, misery and woe your occasion!
Behavior is what I was told to gauge
I am its keeper and its sage
Listen and understand
Feel my rules and plans
This is going to hurt a lot you'll see
But it doesn't represent my morality

health risk

Attention!
Those of you who have lost eyelashes
Whose hair is thinning
Are your breasts small? Or do they sag?
Do all the guys say "You have a flat butt?"
Do women consider you "weak and untough?"
Worry no more! There is an invention
That will improve your life of rags
And ensure that you'll always be winning
You'll avoid the ridicule of beauty's fascists
"You're too fat!" That's what they all say
Don't worry about that
We have a remedy just for you and you
Let's help you grow many a lash
Take these pills three days fast
Those breasts small and aged
Surgery affords them growth; they're perkier too
Forget about your ass's poor display
Inject this into that plateau flat
And watch your vain insecurities fade
A sensitive man you are
Emotions tend to guide you
Inject this and watch machismo lead you
Never again will you succumb to the ladies plan
To call you less than half, a half man
And half-a-man you'll be
All of your fat we'll delete
Now you are a star!
Your hair long and full
Implants of hair from a Spanish Bull
Forget those poison tits you paid for
Those eyelashes allow you to look good blind
At least when your ass explodes
Your man's secure because his dick will implode
And he hides his tears like a man, fine
His scalp now a cow's hide
It's worth the risk

Flinch at vanity's kiss
We get rid of wrinkles too
You know this is beauty and why it's true
Sacrifice your health for the here and now
And look exactly like a man or woman, proud

you better be dying

Do your lungs still work?
Good, help yourself. When you die
Then you can call me

realer than flesh

Watching, listening, watching
Entranced by what you're watching
Reading, imagining, reading
Interpreting, judging and then ignoring
Spellbound by your ethereal world
Created for esteem, managed by self-worship
Farce and arrogance are just as culpable
A world thought to be bereft of tangibility
Physical and true emotional devoutness deemed impossible
Communicating in a distant space
Where all the actions aren't feasible
As simple as they seem
All the words distorted
All the words the same
All the words repeated and exalted
Believed and deified
Then lived, then denied and auctioned
A world where documenting ideas and thoughts
And your whereabouts and activities
Is clearly tantamount to enjoying them or enacting them
Enacting them in the physical world that you dilute
Because nothing exists outside
Your perception of reality
Rather, what you've fabricated
Or what has been manufactured
Acts of gratification born to garner attention
To get people to notice you
Or hate that they do
Forgiving the cries of others
Those who haven't devalued reality
Those who understood the fact
The fact, that if you write it
If you see it
If you heard it
It becomes the reality you always knew
Not something new
It is the reality that you know

Is it realer than flesh?
No!
Despite those who act like so

black face

No offense taken
Tan, coffee brown to shadow black
We love our skin too

spoiled brat

I know how things should be
There should have never been worry
Nor what travails or strains and brings woe
Ideas no one should have ever known or know

Why can't it be my way?
Why? Fucking, why?
This is not okay
Why are you ignoring my cry?

Listen to me!
Listen! I beg of you please!
This is how we'll fix this!
Don't you want agony not to exist?

Why can't it be my way, strong?
Why? Why? Why?
Especially if you know anguish is wrong
Who are you to ignore my cry?

Are you ready to do things how I would?
Okay good!
Ummm... this is how we end misery's taunt
Just give everyone, everything they want

3084

In the 21st century
A great American writer wrote something...
It was moving and characterized all
Humanity forever will be
His stark prose was alarming
Impactful and only told the truth
Prophetic it was
In 2013 he bravely wrote
"Darkness isn't a phase.
It's the latest craze...
Set these days ablaze."
And humanity did, they listened
His work was scathing and scolding
Turning each page intensely singed you
Your hands burning but pages turning
He said that society would crumble
That our souls had been fried
Humanity sustained its trouble
He decried "Hope isn't ours.
It certainly isn't mine.
It's long gone and left with our spine"
The universe he wrote
Was cynical, true
But it was what his brutal honesty knew
The universe closed its vast eyes
And regressed, devolved
And darkness stayed
In every heart alive
Misery unsolved
And happiness broke
And for centuries his proclamation,
"Recognize what you read.
And what you view and digest.
It may become your likeness"
was lived.
Mr. Sheppard you see
Is responsible for our dark history

the "like" button

I want to feel good
Please like my picture, you must
I'll do anything

ephemera

Words are fleeting
Especially when greeting
And as those words had passed
So does their judge
And what you thought to ask
Answered begrudged
All night I write
Today, tomorrow, and forever
Believing in my prose
Knowing that it has to last and that it could never
EVER be forgotten or consigned to oblivion
Every word's might
Must stain the reader's nose
Their tongue must be bitter-ridden
The eyes used to read, confabbed
"My sight has went a-missin' "
Their eyes couldn't touch scopes meager and plain
And blearily read with resigned consent
The works that even I have trashed
You processed what I wrote
And listened to the way it had spoke
You nodded and sighed as if to complain
And my words were never remembered again

watch for danger

Happy-go-lucky
Always with a smile wide
Always touting what he thinks
Of what he perceives
The explanation and reasoning for everything
Finds foundation in his thoughts
He is very intelligent, trust me
His view is always a surprise
And it isn't popular by instinct
I can't understand the thoughts he conceives
But his thinking is interesting
I believe, that his conscience is distraught
It is not what he says that is worrisome
That would be dumb
His happiness belongs to his philosophy
And that's what is scary

common knowledge

I know what they know
We know, I think we all know
We were born to know

daddy to be

I don't make enough money
Job?
This tiny studio for you, your mommy, and me?
Obsessed with the womb I am
How did I grow there?
I've planted you there
This is fucking scary
What if I drop you?
I'm a drunk, it could happen
What if I get lost in the bottle?
Succumb to addiction
And steal food from your mouth?
What if I go to jail?
Your mommy's mood swings...
You will get to know her, you'll see
She's crazy just like me
And I'm afraid you'll be crazy too
I just want to be a good daddy
Failing you can't happen
You're so fragile
Endless potential
Which can only be stagnated by me
Your father
But I will do my best
And you won't know of what worries me
Because I am your daddy

hell is where the heart is

He is singing
His signage is art
And actually, maybe
Jesus put a song in his heart
His elation is evidence enough
A song is there
It is 97 degrees outside
This man sure is tough
Singing his song in the bright sun
A heart in the bright heat, in the fire
Antagonizing the dark
Sharp and high and loud he sings
Even when his lungs had burst
The heat unwavering in its fieriness
He ends his song in thirst

fairly warned

Please, Don't live this out.
Fairly warned, be thee, says I
I predicted this

dramatic license

Those tears aren't real
Down your cheeks they fall
Each one attempting to reveal
Your bleeding trying to dissolve
A heart hiding what is truly felt
You're not serious I can tell
An actor's cries to himself
To garner sympathy that can't be quelled
I nearly believed your character
To be a great actor you aspire
But I can't permit you to lure
My feelings, dissuaded by your act entire
You almost got me to believe
Graciously, please, accept my reprieve

antipathy

I do not like you
I hate what you are about
You suck, you sure do

burrowing

Indiscriminate logic walking towards a large hole in a small mountain
Passing judgment on the towering weeds skipping in the opposite sky
Pruning their limbs to fulfill the wishes whispered by fearful expositions
Walking along a trail of worried and disgruntled foxes and their ambivalence
Two crows nesting on a tortoise swiftly injure three teaspoons of precision
That lied in the meadow to fail the six hawks baiting eleven optimistic warnings
Designed to deter optimism's sixty-six generous fallacies
Who bait those walkers politically chaotic to follow destitute delusions
Safe divisions in measuring six hundred wavering principles calms sedated sloths
Persuaded roses running from the feigning forest tripped on fading aspirations
While dogs dug deep away from shallow ingenuities howling demeaning traits
Bear claws cut idiotic idiocies meant to defy the intelligence of ignominy
Awful oblivion asks ten thousand ants to take solace in grizzly perseverance's fall
Logic walking into the doom of inevitable misunderstandings cave burrowing deeper
Deeper and deeper it burrows hazing insanity unwavering in its prejudice
Unable to escape the nine giraffes peering into a dimension harboring inconsistence
Feeding on the leaves of books that haven't been written by authors never born
Lost in the benevolence of a demeanor stricken by wicked affluences
Only allowed by relaxed intricacy
Fearful insanity awaiting the toll accosted by a tempered imagination
Paralyzed by fatigue unable to dig, unable to concede and unable to give

ennui undo

I have written all
Fatigue will allow me to
What else can I do?

banned books

Combine words in a certain way and some people won't like it
In fact, some people may get offended
For that controversial line has only defended
The existence of thoughts horrible to wit
Maybe certain ways of thought should be disregarded
Certain ideas and ideals were not meant to exist
This way of thinking I resist
Those combinations of words can't be discarded
There are beings suffering
Incest and murder and rape and molestation aren't to words relegated
Racism and misogyny and homophobia and ableism can't be negated
The horrors of humanity won't be erased by your buffering
The freedom that is denied the order of certain words
Is not more offensive than the acts they depict
So words we should never restrict
It is people; it is the universe that is disturbed

the dark matter

I know you hate it
Because it can't be explained
But you know it's there
Light can't penetrate
Nor illuminate its shape
It can't be quantified or measured
But you feel it in your heart
This dark energy amassing
It's deluge swallowing all you believed and could have felt
Affecting all of your thoughts and how you act
Some think you're insane
Others know you are
The rest disregard you
As they do this force that has no true definition
All you know is that you feel it
It has swallowed you

life happens every minute of 24 hours

Slow news day today
For hours on end pundits spoke
About breathing air

suffer in peace

There quietly
On the living room floor
A young boy sits
He hears the slamming of doors
A lot of shouting and screaming
The television can't get any louder
He looks indifferent
This is normal to him
Glass breaking and holes in the wall
A lot of tears running like a lot of blood
But the boy sits stoically
He doesn't slouch, his back is strong
He laughs when the cartoons ask
The young boy just sits and laughs and laughs
At the television and the turmoil

none or 1,000,001

"I would like a beer, please. Cheapest on tap."
I don't have much money
Why do I do this to myself?
I know one leads to many more
I know I have a problem
This time I'm only going to have one
"Thank you."
…
Maybe I'll have one more
Two is a good amount
Two and then I'm done

taking the stage

I have witnessed many people take the stage
Faux actors and actresses and models vying for fame
To be trending or liked
And just like the professionals
They only perform for the camera
I used to believe that people have always been awful
And mourned that cameras were pointed at every single one
But now I know that some people are simply performing
For validation and insecurity and once again for fame
So many women trying to look the same
Enhancing their assets so they feel good about their pictures
Every woman isn't born with a big ass or big tits
But now they all have them
Disregarding the only characteristics that matter in work and in love
Character, heart, mind and personality
Denying their better judgment
The men are much worse
Not only do they encourage women to act and look a certain way
They degrade them for doing so
Both of them fighting only when the camera is turned on
Always against a defenseless opponent who didn't know
That physical confrontation was imminent
Both feigning heartlessness and callousness
Treating death like they are immortal
The whole world isn't a stage
Acting isn't an art form forced upon the human condition
Every human should not share the same wants and beliefs
The body isn't something to disfigure for comfort
Despite the many surgeons who would have you think differently
A fight or a horrible act inflicted upon someone innocent, enjoyed
That I won't enjoy anymore
Please, stop performing
I promise I will

wish to die

I get suicide
You don't want to be here now
Just wait, death will come

"you don't say?" said they

Brevity amorous!
Say what you have to say fast
We must pace this day, porous
More minutes this conversation can't last
They said that?
Who said what?
Oh *They* said those sentences you found apt
Whose name did you cut?
No one's name was cut? You don't say?
They writes and speaks about many interesting things
Knowledge *They* must crave
They has to be a genius, it seems
Quotes by *They* I am always fed
Although, none of their work I have read

your child's future still

Upload that picture
I'm sure your child will love that
On their resumé

i forgot

I couldn't keep holding the past captive
The news has to be to this second fabricated, active
No more space can be committed
To what time has already omitted
What can't be replaced
Is that what happened and it did so true
And this position's hue
Was colored and molded
By the mistakes and ire and triumphs of a yesterday scolded
Retrospect tells great stories, shame faced
My past can't be forgotten
No matter how rotten
I can easily destroy words written for history
But find it hard to destroy the memories

you're responsible, personally

First year of college
And tonight is the night
I forget all of my knowledge
And get piss drunk and maybe fight
This fraternity seems nice
They've invited me and my girlfriends in
Offered us drink after drink
Until our heads start to spin
I start to think
That we have made some new friends
Until confrontation and cries
About when the party should end
The fun we're having is lies
Our thoughts are cloudy and blurred
I'm sorry about what happened, what happened to her

the whole world is the same

Politics is volatile
And I know why
Governing means to try
To align all minds
Most minds
Or as many as possible
To what you believe to be right
As a politician your job description is
To make as many people think
Exactly like you think
You have to persuade them against their own interests
Always against their own prosperity
Think the same
The entire planet will be better
If you think the same as I do
Conflicts only arise when certain interests
Are met with other's resistance (not our shared interests of course)
Everyone needs the same things
Food, water, security, and shelter
You know that is true
So they should listen to me and not her or him
Or you
We're all essentially same
Just let me win the game

reason circles

Only a dream can
Kill another dream. Tell me
This is a dream

the new year knew me

2013 knew me
The same as 2012
2011 predicted I would be
Who I was when 2010 did end
2009 thought I would change for sure
But when it did begin
It knew me just as 2008 did
2007 and 2006
Had hope that my flaws they'd fix
But they soon learned
Just like 2005 and 2004
That changing me is a chore
The year 2014 soon will discover
That it will fail to change me
Just like all of the others

resolved

I gave up on New Years Resolutions a long time ago
The end of the year should not determine when I change
And all those who oppose
That thinking, I think, they're simply deranged
While I don't promise myself metamorphosis
I do like to engage in reflection
Yes, reflection is something I highly endorse and can't resist
Last year had trials from which I am still trying to find protection
So January 1st can't be a clean slate
Last year I judged a lot of peoples' fate
Something I continue to do, it's fun
I can't help but to do so, it's incredible
How I do so with so much blithe
And with a grand sapience full
Causes a delightful fright
I've watched my relationships wither
But the loss of some family and friends
Will not allow my resolve to dither
Something my judgment cannot recommend
Is abjuring that I know who I am and what I have become
But what I know and what I believe
Is that my thoughts may change some
Still, I will not ask for any reprieve
I know that in the new year promises are made
Reading more, working out and being more charitable and nice
Eating better and less, curbing your opinion, more money saved
All things I should strive for and might
But what I have learned in twenty-eight New Years Eves
Is that when attempting a new beginning
The chaotic nature of life derails, and need
Always ends up winning
Even though I judge you for trying now
Keep trying, try and try and try and try
And when misrule is allowed
Your effort no one, not me, not anyone can deny
My foibles, I will fix differently, if I have any
But if your resolve lies in dates, remember there are many

i am "different"

I am the greatest artist
The world has ever seen or known
I do what I want and express myself
How I feel I should
And you all love it
It doesn't matter what I say or do
You'll eat it up, you will chew
I am the greatest artist to ever exist
And of that accomplishment, I am undoubtedly proud
Even though artlessly and honestly
I just appease the crowd

misfortune

Just my luck, I was
Killed, I died in a large crowd
Of cameramen

there is nothing to do in prison but desecrate your flesh

It's dark here
I can see that
It's the only thing I can see
Expansive walls they're out of my reach
Traversing the peril-full scene
I pass through many of them
Nothing is shackling me
I can roam freely
No doors are closed
The air is fresh
And when I'm hungry, I eat
I often get thirsty
Then, I drink
It's just too dark
I don't know if I'm eating water
Or drinking fish
I can't tell if I'm walking on granite
Or running in mud
I can feel the ground
It feels like I sleep in grass
But I can't be sure
Textures make we weary
I want to know I'm eating a rose petal
Or being chased by a grizzly bear
Touch and taste not managed by my eyes, can be deceiving
Nonetheless, I am alive
I get most everything I need
There is just too much darkness
I don't know for sure
But I think I'm in prison

i can't refrain

It is impossible to ignore
This unconscionable song you deplore
It is so disdainful and dreadful
That you must acknowledge it whole
This act sings only odious odes
Notes for which your ears should have never been exposed
Each drum and synth and every snare
Makes you want to pull out your hair
This horrendous song with lyrics hideous
Unearth's every one of your artistic prejudices
Many times the radio station you could have changed
But the melody has you entranced and deranged
"What a god awful song
I can't believe I sung along"

only i can judge me

I hear what they say
God knows what is true, he knows…
He does not know me

ruiner

I'm going to beat you down
Break your spirit
Until you don't believe
Mentally, I'm going to tell you everything you believe is wrong
Why it's wrong
And why you're a goddamn idiot
For ever thinking about something so far fetched and dumb
You might be a little fucking retarded, you're a moron
Emotionally, I'm going to get you attached
No, I'm going to make you dependent upon me
Yes, vulnerable... and unsustaining. Unsustaining is good
I'll make you love me
And you will no matter what I do or say or force upon you
I'll desert you and you'll feel longing an epoch of loneliness
And you'll cry
You'll be glad I'm gone but you'll cry and always remember
Physically, similarly to your thoughts your skin will have scars
Bruises with no intention of fading
Forever discolored from what I've inflicted upon you
That pain there, tattooed on your impeccable flesh
You will believe what I believe
You will interpret like me
A broken spirit

writing makes the world go round

Imagine that your favorite book was never written
What about that essay or constitution?
For those thoughts, I'm sure, you'd still be smitten
And it is possible that what would govern
Is the same as today's destitution
But maybe, easier would those thoughts be unlearned

free air

I can't breathe too well
I desperately need air…
How much, please? Thank you!

i right what i like

Everyone has morals and principals
And they're the same for everyone
So all of our children know what is wrong
And what that means against what is right
There is no nuance
We all know the crux of morality
Treat others like you treat yourself
Or want to be treated by others
Everyone wants to be treated well
And well is defined the same for everyone
The sadists and masochists can even agree

trapped

It is difficult
Living when all you do is
Perform for others

the fate of free will

Let your feelings prevail
Even those with callous intentions
For what is action without will's tales
Wrought from life's many merciful inventions
Insensitive to a life frail
And full of chance's contention
But when chance contends with fate
What is innate?

Fate is not for everyone
To some there is nothing more incidental
Than fortune and its fun
And if their motion is guided by fate's principals
Then their motion would be none
And inconsequential
What they feel didn't have to be felt
But feeling helped

The rest are resigned to their fortune's path
If that pebble in the road becomes a stepping-stone
That you trip over then laugh
What was preached and promised and always known
Is that the rail you couldn't grasp
Because you knew that your hand would miss
The questions that your sanity would ask
Your sanity similarly, couldn't grab

Neither can be left to chance
For fate will not let an escape
Come from a scripted dance
The tale of the tape
And how it knows to prance

Is trapped in free will's freight
And what couldn't be known
Is what was always shown
Free will's fun
Resides in what comes

"it doesn't matter what you do, just do what you love."

Hey kids! I have a very important message to give
It doesn't matter what you love to do
Truly, it won't matter for as long as you live
Always, always, always do what you love to
You, young woman, what do you love?
"I love to ride bicycles."
For life you'll wear a cyclist's gloves
You're going to ride many a-miles
And young man, for what are you forlorn?
"I really love to watch my mom cook. I love to cook too."
A spatula will your hands forever adorn
Many happy stomachs are in your future I view
What about you? And You?
What do you all love?
"I love to read!"
Writer
"I love basketball!
The NBA
"I love animals!" "Clothing!" "Helping people!"
Veterinarian! Fashion designer! Nurse!
"I love to kill things!" "I love to hurt!"

false equivalent

I can't believe that you eat there
The owner hates everyone, all things are his harassment
Don't you know what the owner believes is fair?
And to purchase food from his rotten establishment
Not only means you're supporting him and his curses, all
It also means that you're ensuring the preponderance
Of his forbidding causes, tall
Every dollar you spend there is hindrance
To the movements for social and political progress
So put down that chicken
You truly can't eat that! I stress!
Put it down before racism, addiction, homophobia, child labor, sexism, and classism thicken
Choose more progressive restaurants in which to spend your money
Can I have a piece? I'm hungry

retrospect

For the poet far
In front of those who think that
Being old is cool

the library

There is nothing more I carry
Than this myopic view
A universe of knowledge and learning
Confined in citadels of wisdom
Where religions quarrel in peace
And have to accept criticism and science
A place that brings truth to fiction's stories
And denounces non-fictions facts
Travel to Rome or to CapeTown
Or feudal Japan in one day
Then learn how to build a train
To get you to Guadalajara
Compare today's headlines with those decades old
Human history unfolds behind these walls
And only at the cost of getting there
Free is a wealth of philosophy and comprehension
Because knowledge should always be sought
There is no place like the library
The mean of our understanding
And reason for our collective reasoning
A haven for acumen, an institution of circumspection
The only place to exist that truthfully explains existence
An entire universe of ideas housed
In the greatest information center, our most noble dwelling

you better not laugh

I know it is wrong
But I just could not help it
Hope you are okay

genre exercise

Comedy
No banana peel, no fat man falling or rolling or spinning
Just the Fat Man walking happily along, grinning
Thinking about breakfast, bacon, eggs, waffles, and grits
What is so funny about this Fat Man? Is his weight the schtick?
What is this awful jokes ending?
Goddamn it! We missed him slipping on dog shit

Drama
The Fat Man loses his job, his home, and is now all alone
No help, bad health, no hope wanted to be known
He drowns his woes and hurls into ruination
Fortune's cessation
The Gourmand is rescued from his abyss by what glory is prone
And when happiness shown his diseases ate him

Thriller
Lurking, a lurker. The Fat Man's eyes menacing
The shadows mourn his presence's eerie grimacing
The Glutton walks his slow walk every step with harm's intent
It's the look in his eyes and how mine are cinched
There is a lurker, a stalker who knows all my dealings
He's always following, privacy and security never quenched

Adventure
Tethered to change, a new life the Fat Man seeks
He's tired of the familiar names on familiar streets
The wide-eyed Gorger; his Dodge, dog, duffle, and bindle
Trekking dauntlessly the terrain, and its climates from sweat to kindle
Only crisis of the mind and its philosophy and how they eat
A memory indulged for a lifetime. Embellished, swindled

Mystery
Murders are always most rued
Unless something is abusive to reason and rationality can't be subdued
Who is to blame for this obscene tuition?
What is the culprit's gnarled erudition?
Permanently I must chase who destroyed the reality I knew
I'll start with the Fat Man, get his rendition

Romance
She was just a thought once, a taunt
The Fat Man never could relieve himself of her flaunts
Those quick glances, married to her pulling smile's niche
Reeling he was, gladdened by each glance, bewitched
She loved the Lard like he did her, it was her need, want
Together they were all they ever wished

Life
The Fat Man had laughed and been laughed at
He dove into the depths of obscurity, known only by his masks
Insanity told the Gargantuan to force his past
He gave up then understood that pain wasn't fact
Suspicion grows about his connection to love's asked
Death is only life's tact

decency police

Be decent like network TV
No obscenity, not much cursing. You can flirt. Innuendo and mild sexuality
If you feel the need to be crude
To acknowledge and show a reality nude
You will have to pay for life like violence, fucking and a morality more shitty
Or admire the virtue of the news

nature of hate

The tree grows ripe fruit
Born to be eaten or rot
Without any thought

this is revisionism

Are you sure that it happened that way?
I recall the truth being accepted differently that day
After all this time, history ended with a lie
Are you sure hyperbole or pride aren't your guide?
I don't give a fuck what you say
The German's bombed Pearl Harbor in a Japanese disguise

masochist

I bet your vanity, your nature, never thought of this
Maybe in those pervasive, unknown operations of your mind, persists
An indelible penchant, an evinced desire
To suffer at pain and invalidation's mire
Maybe you are a masochist
Because complaint you find pleasurable, without gripe you don't exist

incapable of guilt

Are you hurt badly?
Well, this is what you deserved
Give me back my knife

i see you hiding

You thought shade would be your cover
But your darkness engulfs the shadows of the trees
And when twilight comes and dusk drives out the sun
I see you through and through, your true view's obscurity
For the moon also refuses to illuminate another
Murkiness is not yours alone, it cannot be owned or won
I see you hiding
For in the dark we see best
You see me here, like I knew you could
We are light's pests
Pessimists who to only darkness abiding
There is no veil that can cloak our good
Come out. It is safe, with me you'll be okay; day or night
And we'll hide together, in plain sight

drones are good

An unintended consequence of drones populating our skies
Is one that science can't explain with its own eyes
Birds seem to be mating with these intelligent machines
And giving birth to robot birds that instinctually delivers things
Another benefit of this new bird/robot breed
Is that they shit energy, they shit batteries

the god of money

God isn't materialistic, of course god isn't
That would go against most religious doctrine
God despises greed and its infamy
The pursuit of fortune for material gains is a sin
Money counts infinitely just as god tends to be
Pursuing money without god makes money distant
So what this all really means
Is that to pursue riches and god
Are essentially two goals that are the same
And maybe it is the practices that are fraud
Simply, it is all a complicated game
That fleeces, beguiles, and demeans
No matter how close you get to it
You'll never touch what's infinite

i do care

All the world's problems are seriously about to be solved
I've found the easiest way and most important way to get involved
With my disdain and my pen I will hoard
The fallibility of humanity that descent humans deplore
I will expose and out these injustices and how they should prevail no more
I care too much for the universe, so apathy I can't explore
I will write about the world's ills and ailments
And all that I lament
Writing my opinion is the greatest action
I truly care, all of my time spent writing misery's caption
Oh shit! What if I write the world into utopia's spin?
What the fuck would I write then
Maybe, I should put down my pen
I may never write again

vacuum

I prefer apples and the "classics" and vegan food
And anyone against my preferences alters my mood
If you don't like apples you must have never had a dad
If you don't read Browning your life is doomed sad
What I like and care about and love and covet won't move
Your opinions are hollow, you're mad!

weirdos in black

Look at these odd birds
Misfits, fucking nutcases
Their skin? No that's them!

story arc

How did this ever begin?
Death's hideous chagrin
From the first breath to blissful ignorance
My hope belongs to another's opulence
If I am to be remembered, bend the narrative, I did win
And greatness I owned it, I didn't rent

what they will say about me after i die

Today, we lay to rest an honorable man
He was convicted of what he couldn't understand
All he wanted was to define words and make them guilty
But learned that when you worship times, filthy
Your jokes and anecdotes and definitions never land
Death finally listened to his command

no credence to rumors

Yes, you are right
I did fuck that goat in its ass, tight
It 'baaahed' like a sheep! My cock too big
Yes, it was very pleasurable for me and it
I am a goat fucker. I fuck goats with all my might
Well, that's what I was told I did

universe forgives all

There is nothing outside of the realm of chaos
Literally, there is nothing, there is no draw
As the universe, I've seen everything that is nothing that is everything
And this I confidently sing
There is no shock or surprise or awe
I don't give a fuck, that's what I mean

news does not mean truth

BREAKING NEWS! Today,
The world is going to end
Just after this break

prepare for the big one

It only takes three seconds
To teach this important and life affirming lesson
One of these days we will shake and shake and shake and shake
And then California will split from her country mates
Although, there is no exact day or even certainty, just guessin'
If you want to survive a huge fucking land mass violently drifting into the
Pacific Ocean, an earthquake kit you should make

rape is nirvana

This is desire
And it didn't have to say a word
I was wanted and needed and taken
Stolen and pillaged and I knew I wanted it
I see your hands raised
I am not alone
We feel this way, ruined, because we were wanted
Like it was necessary
It was necessary
This is bliss
Knowing the torture of hell

always within reach

All of your attention always and instantly
If you want to be my love, next to me
You must provide that security
When I contact you, you better always respond quickly
That is how I know you give a fuck about me
Fastest means you care more. I won't be slow either, you'll see

forget alcoholism

When you drink a lot
You're only sober a few times a day
You drink and drink and your brain rots and rots
And those times you cannot remember or replay
Are distraught
And here to stay

i love an artist

"Good grief!
I can hardly speak
His poems are worthy of no words
As if they were never written
All they needed were faces
Not comatose, faces that would display emotions
Emotions that could never be known
Because thousands of pages of blank paper
Don't mean anything but the death of trees
My love writes all night
I summon him to bed and he denies me
Because he cannot forget his thoughts
Or create without my silence
I'm sorry that I love you" – L.C.

soul for sale

On the market right now is a premium soul
It is comprised of a generous heart and very discerning mind
This is a one time only price, half of the whole
Just be strong in body because it will take its toll
You will never consume a soul of this kind
Never mind, I think I'll keep mine

it's fun to escape

This realm is boring
I grow weary of its elusion
No longer can I wade through life snoring
Acknowledging boredom's intrusion
But there is this place soaring
Find your way, by any means, to this illusion

criticism schism

What a prism!
A haven for skepticism and opinions dissenting
It is comforting to know that what is thought of thought
Will be challenged and disproved
Only to be adopted and practiced
Persuasion isn't absurd
Here, division isn't denied, suppressed or hated
Here, you are free from the tyrants who tell
That thought must be to them aligned
Your ideas won't face the wrath of Draco
There is no ego or want to be right
Or a need to control or gain influence
Here, your ideas won't be appraised
What an amazing spectrum of sincere objectivity!
How do I get the fuck out of here?

i love you so much

What you think you are saying and how it is heard
Are not the same to me
The innocence you intended to project
I interpret as deadly malignity
I heard what you said and can define those words
You just said them with a fervid neglect that I can't respect

i know what you're thinking

I feel the same way
Yes, you are completely right
Did you say something?

a relative minute

I hit the snooze button one more time
One more minute of sleep and I'll be fine
Just this one-minute, glorious
And I'll be ready for the workday, laborious
Rest is what I need and its relief
Eyes closed for a moment brief
That minute was not enough to appease me
Even though that minute became one hundred eighty
How can three hours pass like a minute, swift?
Now I am late for my shift
I think I'll go back to bed
Another minute of sleep at my job's risk
Will my restlessness ever be fed?
Time is bullshit

father

For my family I live and breathe
All I do is for you two
That is not honorable, true
Honorable is the man who concedes
Everything that he once believed and its fallacy
Ready I am, to protect and provide and never get my due

that's not me... anymore

I have no answer for my past
I said what I said and did what I did
I learned and loved and loved to laugh
With all the people who assumed that success is rigged
For some reason I felt I had been denied something
I use to feel that life's failings are due to things dumb
Processes that were coerced by a societal justice fleeting
But now I know that the fallacy in my complaints
Was acknowledging the power I was never bestowed
So who I am now damaged and quaint?
I understand that there is nothing I am owed
I used to be lazy
All I did was claim that I had been maneuvered to be low
Because of my qualities incidental, just like I was taught and told
What I now know
Is that my life has always been by me controlled

brought to light

Shadows are scary
Because what they hide
Maybe hideous and pernicious
But still, I am interested and suspicious
I sought what darkness hid
And my thoughts it did scar
But who's to blame for my cognition now morbid?
Darkness didn't ask me to seek its heart, horrid
Oh, what horror!

the sin of writing such words

Jesus repented today
Sin had befallen this entity
Contrition the mission
"Sorry for being created and abused
Sorry for being used
Sorry for the propagated truths
That only lied"

you have it all figured out there buddy

I know what human nature is supposed to be
So come to me if you want to be injustice free
You can easily teach people not to be awful
One. Two. Three. And hate unlawful
All the "-isms" of Liberalism will cease
And the universe will know an unknown peace
All you have to do is protest and march and write
Just fight the good fight
And what is entrapped in the recesses of a dark mind
You will find
You will heal
You will kill
Soon discrimination will have no offerings
Because my methods have much to say
I know you can't quantify the progress or see a dent in suffering
But it's working, for our suffering got a holiday

they are not better off

I hope you're comfy
This presentation decides
That money is pride

sins of the father

Son, when my sins come a'knockin'
Please heed this advice if any from me, your father
Even if the house is shaking furiously, a'rockin'
Ignore their trespass, their bother
Listen to me this one time, if never before
Don't open that Goddamn door!

numbers be lying

Did you know that when you eat feces, you die?
We here at Numbers took a survey
Nine out of every ten people won't deny
That ten out of ten people who eat these turds will perish away

Their breath will be damned by pungency
And become exceedingly caustic to their own nose and mouth
Which will both explode with an intense redundancy
As if the results were ever in doubt

Our sample size is still incredibly small
This all may be just a minuscule aberration
We won't stop until we feed human waste to all
Who wants part in this groundbreaking experimentation?

Don't let the ten dead bodies be a deterrent
You sir and you ma'am be willing to take the risk
I've done it and I've only had to deal with breath abhorrent
Oh, and being full of shit

validate me

Save me from the tyranny of self
My thoughts, my opinions, my experiences
Tell me that it's okay to think this way
I won't do anything unless you feel it's okay
I love what you like and the differences
This is my will and my health

Validate me my friend
Approve of me again and again
Validate me, please!
It's you I must appease

I know what I said in earnest back then
But now I've changed my mind to yours
Now you should have no problem accepting me
I now see exactly what and how you see
Forgive me if my eyes detour
Just know that your preferences win

Validate me at once!
And endorse our united front
Validate me before I dither
Before I wither

the drunk writer

From ancient engravings on the walls of caves
To the finest plume dipped in the finest ink
The typewriter and then Word and other software
The writer has relied on a drink fermented
To loosen their mind so from their hands flows
Words that pray to the universe and its effigy
The relationships fractured and bodies destroyed
Because to share the thoughts they thought with all of eternity
Numbed or had to be constantly celebrated
Or maybe it is understood
That the writer has to be drunk
To believe that someone
Will actually care about what they have written

trends change

I've been trending down
For a long fucking time now
I am still falling

the network snarl

I've been looking for great kitchen knives
The best on the market to cut vegetables and meats
Review after review I revised
Left me with too many choices to seek

One reviewer posted a link to a website refreshing
It was a grand search engine that didn't hide results
Knives galore! Many more choices for guessing
Their history and their uses from food to occult

I stumbled upon a review by someone completely insane
It was written by an assassin that only used knives on his job
He felt that rifles, pistols with silencers, and piano wire were inane
But shared links to those who used those tools and their 'more efficient' facade

He used a blade that couldn't be searched on Google
It also could not be bought on eBay or Amazon
When you search its name there are no results to doodle
In fact, that knife doesn't exist, my spelling suggested wrong

But there is review after review about this blade
Sharp enough to sever a man's head in one swift swipe
Strong enough to cut her bones without struggle or rage
With graphic video displays so you read the review right

Yahoo, Bing, I asked Jeeves, and I Googled and Googled incessantly
Because the existence of that knife I couldn't believe
But no website out of billions had ever known that knife's discrepancy
That knife I couldn't believe

It arrived in the mail one Sunday afternoon
This glorious blade to gut my chickens
As I carved I couldn't help but swoon
And wonder about what else online is hidden

I traversed the deep web all day and all night
No going to work or sleeping or even eating
Just consuming the depths of the human condition's perverse rights
And why this capricious depravity I'm seeking

I waded through those dark depths
Filled with the certain destitution that possesses much of humanity
And why these websites and thoughts should be buried deeper and unkept
I then feared that all I sought to know was meant to control me

the preeminent measurement

I want more hours in the day
More minutes and seconds too
I wish one day saw at least three moons
And sunrises weren't wedded to the amount of sunsets
Twenty-four hours I fret
In fact, most of time is doomed
For it is dependent upon breaths new
And how many happy birthday's you can say

I fear that time doesn't measure productivity
But it only measures decay
It defines insecurity
That relies upon breathing and sustenance
That never realizes the importance
Of what it means to be
Time only measures our dying day
And our fear of that activity

Restricted by time's scope
And its dim valuation
All those minutes that felt like weeks
The hours of fun that passed like milliseconds
Only dispute time's essence
Time is weak
And can only be useful in measuring deterioration
I understand why we tell time, I hope

nate, this is how i'd live if i were a good person

kindness
"Can I borrow some change? Please, can you lend me some change?" said the homeless man.
I told the man, "Ask me again."
"Can I borrow some change, please? Please, I beg your generosity, can you lend me some change?"
"You aren't asking the right question. Please sir, ask me the question again and tell me what you truly want from me."
"Forget it, you fucking asshole!"
"I'm the asshole? You asked to borrow some change, to borrow money knowing your inability to pay me back, knowing you'd probably never see me again..."

Generosity
"I now understand what you were asking. I apologize for calling you an asshole. I am the asshole. Can I please have some change sir? Thank you."
"No," I said as I turned my back on the homeless man and walked away.

Fairness
"Let's do something tonight, babe," your mother suggested.
I answered mirroring her vigor and anticipation, "Yes Bella, let's do something tonight," I then asked the obvious question, "What do you want to do?"
"Let's go to the movies or lets go play billiards." Both activities we love to do and love to do together.
"Why can't we do both?" I told her. "Let's go to a matinee then go to a bar. We haven't been out together in a long time."
"Okay babe, that sounds like a great plan. What's out that you want to see... Uh oh, Nathaniel's crying. I think he's getting sick."
"Well, I'll see you when I get back Bella."
"Where are you going, Jonathan?" Your mother asked sternly in her angry tone, you know her angry tone.
"To the movies and to a bar to play billiards."

Humility
Nathan if there is one thing that you should know about dear old dad it's the fact that I am the greatest writer in history. My poetry is all enduring and will be studied in the world's greatest universities for centuries. I captured the time in which I live, the time in which you were born, with the utmost honesty. I captivated every reader who ever laid his or her eyes upon my remarkable and effulgent works. For my poems and short stories and everything else I have written have been held with the greatest esteem and will be quoted with the great works of the English language's great antiquity.

Honesty
No one reads my work, Nathaniel. My work is the ramblings of an alcohol fueled, unhealed sycophant. This would be axiomatic to anyone who read my work. No one cares.

Integrity
"Do you always write what you feel?" your mother asked me once, "I mean, do you mean all of the things that you write in your poems?"
"I only write when I feel." I responded, "Which just so happens to be my every waking moment. That's when truth happens... I mean it at the time I write it, otherwise I wouldn't have written it."
"I love you Jonathan," your mother said lovingly, her eyes full of hopeful despair.
"I love you too Lizette," I responded in kind, "It's true. I have it written here somewhere."

Purpose
"Jonathan can you please do this. Jonathan you need to do that. Jonathan you're not doing that correctly. Jonathan stay home, Jonathan you cannot go out with your friends. You cannot buy new clothes or shoes. You have to pay bills, and work, and listen. You have to provide now. You have to take care of your body and your mind. Stop drinking so goddamn much. No more cursing or being crude..." that's what everyone has told me.
"I'll do whatever you say," I reply.

Sensitivity
There are so many stray dogs and cats in our neighborhood. Every street that I cross from Soto to St. Louis is with an animal that doesn't have a home. "Kitty please be careful crossing the street, you too doggy. When you make it across the avenue safely there will be food and water. I am sure of it because I placed it there. You can collect energy to survive another day." How do people not care about these animals who are only victims of a society humanity created? I can't believe this ass-fucking-hole is approaching me again. "Get the fuck out of here you bum. I told you I don't have any fucking change."

Self-Discipline
A pen and pad are left alone. They sat new and unused in the path I walked. Like an omen, the machina, the universe's way of telling me that I am to be a great writer and the only thing I have to do is commit my bad thoughts to paper... Gleefully, I kept walking.

Patience
"Nathaniel can you please stop crying? Your diaper has just been changed. Nathan you have just been fed. Nate please tell me what is wrong. Please son! I beg of you. If you don't tell me son, I can't help you. Otherwise, I'll be forced to listen to your beautiful cries all night. I can listen to your beautiful cries all night."

Forgiveness
If I show you anything you can't forgive, if I do anything you can't forgive, when you experience the horrors of your father's mind, of a man deranged. You don't have to forgive me. You can hate me for eternity. You can piss and shit on my grave and denounce my work, my life, and my worth. You can deny me and accept your conception as immaculate as predestined and ordained by a god or by a universe of chaotic possibility. Always, always, always, forgive yourself, Nathaniel please forgive yourself.
And if you find it in your heart to forgive me, please note that your father has no clue what it means to be a good person

denial

I'm not an alcoholic
I'm a connoisseur
Look at my shelf, you will learn
That I've tasted and enjoyed many whiskeys/whiskys
From Kentucky to Ireland, Tennessee, Japan to Scotland
Many more have been represented on my tongue
All I can remember are the joyous frolics
And all of the truths that I'd unearth
Each taste from each barrel churned
Has been more pleasure than I can conceive
It's all that I demand
For relaxation, work, and fun
Do you have money to lend me?
All of these bottles are empty

cursed since birth

I'm the luckiest person ever born
Fuck what you say
It isn't evident?
Not at all?
I'll prove it to you
...
...
You don't know anything

censorship? what the hell are you talking about?

Did you hear about what just happened?
Something awful happened to innocent people
I never perceived this asshole as violent
As a man, as a real man I say
That this means that the greater society is awful
Every person that lives and breathes

Has been influenced by another's creativity
We all have trouble distinguishing fantasy from reality
Especially those people who tell stories with moving pictures
They'll never realize
Their fucking lies
Storytelling is humanity's greatest tradition

Morals are defined and taught or denied
But why aren't paintings similarly chastised?
They can be just as moving and drastic
Photographs frozen in horror's space
What about all the books those photographs inspired?
That school rampage can't be influenced by a news article

Nor a painting or photograph or a bird chirping
It had to be film, because he couldn't have just awoken
And felt like killing everyone on earth that day
Everyone is born with the purity of heaven
That is how humanity has been programmed
You can only learn how to demean and destroy

We don't learn how to be nice
It just happens
Kill all the killers for worship
Paint pictures of their photographs
Sing all your songs for them and name your band their name

Word after word written to become their film
That taught the killers to kill
And commanded us to kill the killer
Please stop creating things
They influence inherently good people
To do inherently bad things

All artists must die

moral superiority

I'm sure that I'm right
And you know that you are wrong
Are days black or light?

i have a complaint

Thank you for listening
What a shame...
I cannot believe what I continue to witness
How can humanity be so intolerant, still?
It is 2014 and times have changed
And to think with prejudice and bigotry
As archaic as they are
And how they prove people moronic and ignorant
Means something to someone
I'm tired of being judged, don't judge me
I'm only reacting to what I was taught and see
And how I feel and interpret what the senses give me
I care so much about this ignorance
And as it exists I will always pay attention to it
I will shout it down and let everyone know I hate it
My art will be consumed with changing their minds
Because it hinders my breath
It takes away from my happiness
I want everyone to accept everything about me so badly
People always questioning the definitions I challenge
The life I lead
I won't stop until everyone accepts me
Okay I'm done
Thanks for your time
I'll grab the next person in line

black love

Oh yes, there is no love with more beauty
You and I, us, born of the same kind
Pure forever. That is what this means and all I see
Forever you and me
Even though I am blind
I can see the dark depths of your mind

shaken

I can't believe this is happening
This midget man has dwarfed me
Fear spawning and grown
My legs are weak and buckling
He only wants my phone, to use my phone
At least that's what he asked
"We can do some gangster shit dog or
I could just take it from you."
Shaken by what the situation could be
It's too early
I'm on my way to work and all I need is change
All I need is bus fare
I open the refrigerator door and grab two waters
Two liters for three dollars
When I close the door there stands a bald headed man
He was much shorter than me
He was much shorter than my girlfriend
He was three feet taller than my son who has 25 inches
The question was asked and I said no
Again and again I said no
"Nah, you can't use my phone."
"Why not?"
"I don't let anyone use my phone."
I paid and got 'Cash Back' enough money for a day pass
"We can do some gangster shit dog or
I could just take it from you."
I handed him my phone
Shaken by what the situation could be
My first thought was to punch him as hard as I could
But he had five friends outside
I thought about my girlfriend and my son
And what if he had a weapon, a knife or a gun
My second thought was if he ran off with my phone
I would have to fight him
I was never taught to back down, you fight
You don't let anyone take anything from you
Unless you want nothing

I thought about my family again
And how he probably has nothing to lose
My family needs me because I need them
Her and him, and if my life ends over a phone
A new start could never begin
He told me he was educated too
That he had read some psychology book
Assigned to him by some class
At East Los Angeles Community College
I didn't understand
He gave me back my phone and left the store
I left the store too and my two water bottles
Fear is paralyzing
At the bus stop I was still trembling
And thinking about what could have happened
Fear is paralyzing
Glad I decided to make it to work on time

the death of amateurism

I am as good as you
The same equipment we use
In fact, my tools are much, much better
So is the quality
You see my resolution?
I can't wait until I can afford the content solution

to live and die in heaven

Only Angel's here
Los Angeles is Heaven
Only Angel's here

your heart is showing

There is a pool of blood at your feet
I can see your chest exposed
Your skin severed and rib cage divided in half
You're still breathing, heavy but discreet
I think you're dying the death you've always opposed
Thanks for the laughs

father's day

I will do my best to ensure
That my son will always know
The half I gave him

I will read his cards
And love all the gifts he gives
If I get any

If he resents me
Sadness is all I would know
And he will see it

I am here, you see?
All your thanks and agony
Will always find me

the sign was blurry

What did that sign say?
Oh well
This road is bumpy as hell
And there are many, too many, tolls along the way
Where is this road going, can you tell?
What the fuck did that sign say?

my second poem about seattle

Over 300 days of sun
Actually, I'm sure many more days it has won
No cloud cover
Just brightness and rays one day after the other
I embrace and absorb the tyranny of the everlasting star
That only recognizes sunshine's scars
My home is a sun temple
Where feelings are simple
I was born where the gloomy days are infinite
Until that one sunray shines definite
I would feel happy and understand
That clouds must be damned
Basking in the sun and how it is favorable and warm
Then drained by its unbearable swarm
This task is all I ask
Please clouds, kick the sun's ass
Bring some rain with you

jamais vu

Repeat
Again it repeats
That day
The other awful days
Stark and vivid, pain full
I could never forget the lull
Until I do it right
I'll fight
Yes, forever a fighter
For months, years and seconds
I will fight with this weapon
When I fail, in the end
I can always pretend
That it's something I recommend

honoring the dead

It feels really good
To apologize to you
Now that you are gone

save the clouds

An infinite amount of storage?
This can't be true
All I have to do is give money to you
Ten terabytes could never do
And even if I'm as poor as porridge
I can afford this
One dollar a month
The most vital information and memories
Everything I've written, my history
Is preserved in these clouds of mystery
You will truly feel like a dunce
If you don't scan your photo prints, your gist
Make sure when you're done
You burn the original ones
Banish what you've captured, your growth and fun
To the cloud's mist
Don't you need room to move?
Why crowd your home with artifacts
Things with no tact
In fact,
I'll transfer your pics and your groove
They'll last forever, no doubt
Until the sun comes out

truth: there's an app for that

I think I know what you're thinking
"How can an 'app' tell me the truth?"
Why wouldn't that be what you're thinking?
Truth has been sought for centuries
Is my lover cheating on me?
Is kale really that good?
And of course, where's god?
Well my app will tell you all of that
It will deny your perspective
And all that you hold true
Because you're a goddamn fool!
My application tells you all the universe beholds
And why it is to be
And how the truth is something most never see
Download it now in the iTunes App Store and Google Play

tricksters

You were going to govern?
What a fool I have been
I actually voted for your win
Another lesson learned
What you say versus what you'll do
Will never be true

recycle me

I am trash
No recyclable parts
But please help me last
Help me become a salvageable art
This is not some lark
Reuse me, fast

force your art upon me

Walking along I see
Murals all around me
I hear music blasting from cars
Photographs in storefronts
Statues in sculpture gardens
All begging for admiration

you read that right

You read very well
Didn't they write that today?
And it became true

blessed

I have always had trouble with my "blessings"
Because it seems that to be "blessed"
Means that you're measuring your success
Against others and their "unfortunate" trappings
Am I blessed to not have bombs being dropped on my head?
I am blessed because I won't starve to death?
Or because today I am not dead?
Those are reasons to be blessed?
I am blessed because I have breath?
Because I have shoes?
And you're blessed because you do too?
How come my feet can't be as naked as they were born?
Would I be eating if the unblessed weren't starving?
Most likely I would engage in food porn
And my belly fat would still be enlarging
I simply refute that my "fortune"
Has to be measured against the perceived "misfortune"
Of others
I am not "blessed" and neither are you
Because if death is the only thing that is true
And truth is something that is sought more than most
Than the shoeless, famine stricken person's blessings we should boast
Don't dodge those bombs

intelligent design

Paley's watch and the time it tells
Has a brilliant design, it certainly isn't a stone
It isn't granite or things deemed lifeless
It intricately measures time and its complexity
Like when we grow old the tree stays young
Even if you don't understand the ways of trees

You can't deny their architecture
Or how the growth of trees
Don't hinder the growth of the grass or surrounding flowers
That feed the deer and cattle
Whose carcasses decay and feed maggots and buzzards
That nature has been intelligently designed

Like the watch, that tells arbitrary time
Arbitrary because if it is six o'clock here
Why isn't it six o'clock in every hemisphere?
The watch is dumb without more hands
Just as the tree can't be smart if it's a log
If it becomes a dead house

Does nature work like the clock?
Every seed planted by the bees pollinating
Feeds the buzzard's beak?
Did the buzzard's creator also create the watchmaker?
Relying simply on their omnipotent acuity?
That design is awful

Watches were designed to change time
Trees were designed to be used
Magnets for those thirsty or hungry
Or used by those selfish creatures who need shelter
They were designed for exploitation
For every breath taken by life here

Owes a debt to the breaths of the trees
For even a tree in famine
Still breathes until it withers
Its final gasps, life for the buzzard to eat
Those creatures laid underneath the shade of barren branches
Feeding the buzzard until its wings weak from hunger

And that is why time and design are equally complex
Not simply teleological
And if you don't understand that and know
That time had run out, outdated, was never defined
If you knew that the organism that ate the buzzard and finished off the tree
Were resigned to existence without time

The tree died and so did the buzzard and the flowers, like the grass
Then the rains came and the bees and the sun
Made the flowers grow
More buzzards were born, and more beautiful trees
The prod and void of that mysticism
Is simple empiricism?

Knowledge isn't something told
It is something gained or waited upon, endured
It doesn't appear out of no where
Like the watch
The watch is dependent upon an owner
A creator

To profess what each hand says
But is it like the growth of a tree or flower?
I don't have to mold or fuse or define a flower
I just watch it grow
Would an intelligent designer allow
For its creation's anarchy?

To be what it wanted to be
To love and enforce theology?
What is the time?
Not Los Angeles time
I'm in London
I'm in Sudan and Indonesia

What is the time?
Does the flower still abide?
I'm glad it is finally the same
You're late and the sun died
Some flowers didn't bloom
Patience doomed

Because the clock's battery died
What is happening now?
Ignorance is happening at this time
How did the watch or the stone come to be?
Without you fucking me or me you?
There had to be a mover, a maker, with smarts and dignity

Did you hear that the sun died?
And the watch was fixed
Tick tock, tick tock
...
...
Tick tock, tick tock
Tick tock, tick tock
Almost out of it

listen! listen! listen!

"ARE YOU SURE YOU'RE UNDERSTANDING ME CORRECTLY?
I HAVE TO YELL FOR YOU TO HEAR ME!
I DON'T GIVE A DAMN ABOUT WHAT YOU'RE SAYING
I COULD CARE LESS ABOUT HOW YOU FEEL!
FUCK YOU! FUCK YOU! FUCK YOU!
I NEVER WANTED TO BE AROUND YOU!
HOW HAVE YOU DRIVEN ME TO THIS POINT,
WHERE ALL I CARE ABOUT IS DYING?
I HATE YOU WITH MY ENTIRE BEING!
I FUCKING HATE YOU, YOU BANE, YOU NUISANCE
YOU INDOMITABLE FORCE FIELD OF IGNOMINY
A PERSON WHO CONSUMES ALL OF MY DISDAIN"
...
Wait a second...
What did you say? I wasn't paying attention.
Can you repeat it please?

outrage

Why is everyone
Offended by her actions?
I found them funny

gaza fried chicken strip

On the menu today
Are a landless people
Wrangled onto this farm
This inhumane reservation
Made because those powerful and pale
Decided to atone for their late reaction
Religion aside
No diet ordained or ordered
This dish is the exception
Kosher or not they feast
And forget what they were purposed to believe
Discord and disharmony, mayhem and murder
All because of the belief
That this region is owed to you
So you farm and expand and farm and farm
And fry and fry
And only worry about your sides
And telling all of the lies

i'm so…

Goddamn lost in life
That I look upon my past for validation
Maybe what did happen will suffice
It will help me deal with future trepidation
With my poor reputation
And the things about myself I dislike

a.s.a.p.

When are you coming home?
Can you please hurry?
You'll be home as soon as possible?
That better mean right now
You didn't say never
So I'll wait forever

general lies

Every man thinks about sex every two minutes
And every woman wants every thing
How can those not be true?
They are as true
As blacks and their propensity for thieving
What about whites and all of their benefits?

Gay men will molest your straight son
Latinas are hot as flames and their attitudes too
Lesbians hate all men like feminists do
And you're a thug, an idiot, a criminal with all of those tattoos
And no job will ever hire you
You're fat because you eat tons

I don't know about you but I'm tired
No matter how many don't do something
The fallibility of one monster, one liar
Speaks for a population and what they mean
You represent exactly how they act
Your mannerisms, your unique beliefs, your tact
Generally, I wish I were a General in control of your narrow pride
In front of my firing squad you would lie
For what you generalize

women at the bar

My girlfriend complains too goddamn much
"So does my wife, she never shuts the fuck up!"
All she does is point out what I'm doing wrong
And doesn't understand how I'm being strong
"Same here man, she doesn't understand,
That I could leave her and our kid's plan."
I hate being beholden to her groove
And all that I ever do must be by her approved
"I'm a man goddamn it!"
Aren't we? And we don't owe our ol' ladies shit!
Let me enjoy a beer in peace please
"Her we can't always appease."
I can't wait to be free from her, to be alone
"After this drink I have to go home."

new citizenship: bye bye transplant hypocrite

Why did you move here?
Los Angeles is my home
Get the fuck out, now!

death-full

Death always means something to the living
Let us infer the plain of no breathing
Let us ponder what it's like to never think
And for this cause let us sink

Let us not worry about what happens after this certain event
Can we live and die without the need to invent?
Because if you know what I believe
Then life will be a breeze

I do care about dying
I'm not here to project lies and lying
But what happens when I pass...
Are thoughts I can't have
For when I'm entranced by death's stare
My lifeless, death-full corpse won't care

nuisance

It never hurts to be cautious
Trusting people is too scary
And makes me nauseous
So I have to be chary

stop telling me that you're asking

You know you can't do what I'm doing
That's why you're asking me to do it
Do you have the know how?
No!
Would you take too long?
Yes!
What a horrible job
You're asking me to do
I bet you're glad you can't

nathan's smile

Keep smiling baby boy
I love your gums and how they peek past your lips
You have your mother's smile
So big and so gleeful
One of those smiles that happiness frames
When I come home from work
Tired and beaten, mad and frowning
I look into your eyes
You look back into mine
Then you flash your gums
Then your mom shows her teeth
Then I realize my fatigue and why I am beaten
Then I smile

artificial intelligence

I don't quarrel with the programming of machines
If they're programmed to take humanity
Or decide to with their free will
Let their creator's blood be the first to spill
Actually, I hope they kill all of those who frantically
Express their brain's superior genes
Idiots

my son's mother

Hate has never been stronger in my mind
Hate has never existed as durable in my heart
As it has for my son's mother

She forced love upon me
All of my being, all of my wants and needs
Don't mean shit!

What I feel has no definition
Because of her
She killed me for him, my son

I can see it in her eyes
He's her greatest lover
She loves him more than me

But now that I think about it
I love him more than I love her too
And we love him together the same
I hope that was his aim
If I love you too hard Nathaniel, your mother is to blame

spineless

I noticed today
That hiding is all the rage
You invertebrate

hard head

Nothing can penetrate that massive mind
It refuses to learn
And the spine
This impervious brain spurns
Knows everything ever learned

Don't think this mind stupid
The knowledge it acquired
Is only inspired
By the wisdom of cupid
Now I'm certain this mind is doltish or tired

For the know it all
And the preferences they spout holy
Is theirs to call
If a mind dissents boldly
Their feelings fall
And they espouse a mind small

you can't drive

That is a fantastic idea!
Let's go after it, let's make it happen
We have to get there right now
Oh fuck...
Your car has no engine
We can take the bus
You're broke?
We can walk
You're lazy?
Well, I'm parked over there
Call me when you wake up

lumina

I'm sorry that you
Can't understand my protest
Light is too damn bright!

sunken with the ship

"We must abandon this place
The costs are too high"
You're a disgrace
Talent you'll find by and by

But not like here
You think graduates from top schools
Want to move to where your costs endear?
You all are fools!

This is California goddamn it
If film leaves, if porn leaves
We're prepared, we're fit
The benefits of the eastward move deceive

Leave us here
To die and parish like starving buzzards
We need water simple and clear
But dry springs we'll discover

This is California goddamn it
If it falters and is pillaged by foreign counties
Our soils are like our minds, infinitely rich
And ripe with the lifeless dead, drowning

language's spirit

The body of language is in shackles, finally
Since we all have defined the same we've been trying
To catch Language and its damned diction
Since the creation of fiction
Language is charged with agreeing to a word's use
Then changing the words meaning
Even when its use is based in that leaning
"It hurts the law, it builds pride in poets, and writers are just confused!"
"I truly don't understand what you just said."
The spirit of Language can't be crippled
I accept that you mean that this way,
"What else is there to say?"
Language would always say and smile
"You can lock me down but you will all soon agree with my rationale...
Let me be free!"

the fallacies of the scorned forlorn

You will hear me, I said that I love you!
I hate that you don't believe that I do
Why are you always picking on me?
If you say one more word
I'm going to beat your ass

I'm sorry, I am stressed
Hours upon hours I work
And each of those hours are days of agitation and agony
Please forgive me. I am only human
I need rest, please understand

This is necessary for me and you
And for everyone around us too
We can't be and never should have been
It was awful for society
It was awful for you and me

I don't even know why I bothered to love you
What benefits did I receive?
You dumb ass piece of shit! You dumb bitch!
Trickster, demoness, lying cunt motherfucker!
That's why this has to be

If you really love me
You'd be here, right now with my son
You would forget about what I did
Every child needs a father!
We've never had one

The universe wants us to be this way!
They want me to go crazy
You too, they've already drove you mad
This isn't normal for us
God planned it this way, that motherfucker

Admire the beauty of our child
We should have more beautiful children
You don't want to be around me or fuck me?
I don't want to fuck you too?
Do it for the kids

I said that I love you!
Trust me, believe me, it's true!
I wouldn't lie or deceive
And dinosaurs walked the earth in 1492
Again, I love you

scared to feel because i hate it

I do not like this
Feeling this way, I fear it
I hate that way, too
I'll hide behind this mask
I won't feel... I won't!

toothbrush

RING! RING! RING! RING! RING!
RING! RING! RING! RING! RING! RING!
Okay, I am up
I work today, don't I? FUCK!
I have to hurry
My toothbrush was pink, I thought
I forgot, it's blue
Why is it blue? Pink it was
She would always know
Now I understand, She's gone
And took my toothbrush

you feel sick too often

Quit complaining, please!
We are all going to die
Hypochondriac

i am valuable

"You're fucking worthless
No benefit to my life you are
What have you ever done for me?
You aren't shit Jonathan!
What the fuck have you done for me!"
Nothing
"Just like you!"

memorial

I am not a painter
But I needed a release
Another release
I love what I do
But I needed something new
A novice at best
I love the canvas
A new anchor

what i miss the most

Her face was flawless
Her lush lips frame chipper teeth
So plump... oh her kiss!
Her lips more than anything make my heart beat
But her eyes
Her eyes are piercing
Round and brown, boisterous and beautiful lies
She bites my nose ring
Her smell
Always sensuous and sweet
Her voice frail
I miss anything she said to me
Her body
Oh my... her stomach and arms
Her hands, ass, legs, armpits... her nostrils were godly
Oh her smile's entrancing evil charm
...
Fuck it
What I truly miss the most are her tits, her pussy

evolution human

The mind is power
Don't react on its instincts
Common sense is key

nate's cries

Are you hungry Nathaniel?
Please eat your food
We're in a crowded restaurant
Don't be rude son, don't be rude
Do you need your diaper changed?
I just changed you Nathan
I'll change you again
Listen to your mother Nate
Listen to me Nathaniel
I know you want something
You need something
And I'll search high and low
For your wants because they're mine
But please stop crying all of the time
It's beautiful, I love it, I miss it
Then I hear it and die
Your screams
LOUD! Protecting your mom
Your screams
LOUD! Protecting me
Your screams
I will never forget
And how you looked at me teary eyed
I will never forget
Your mother's tears
And how she looked at me teary eyed
With you in her arms she walked away
Your cries
Haunt my silence

soul-less

I remember constructing this card
Scissors, construction paper, and glue, a few markers
My soul was promised
It was possessed
Someone owned it
But it isn't hers or hers
It isn't mine
It isn't

i cannot sleep

Two hours, four hours, six hours
Alarm clock, 'RING! RING! RING!'
Get the fuck out of bed it sings
"FUCK! SHIT! I QUIT! I JUST WANT TO SLEEP!"
Sweating, the foot of the bed is your head
The head of the bed, your head
There is no way you'll get comfortable
Damp sheets and no rest
Stressed
You arrive to work dragging
Your eyes low
"FUCK! SHIT! I SHOULD HAVE QUIT A LONG TIME AGO!
...Did I say that aloud?
I thought I dreamt it"

miss universe

Please look at me world
No one is more beautiful
Every planet too

half-life

The half-life of sperm
When you beat your dick a lot
Is a quarter-life

the great western forum

Some crowds are big
Most of the crowds are very small
But the huge crowds some acts garner
That some people earn
Are magnificent and majestic to see
Watch them move in unison their bodies and mouths
Chanting an opinion that they share
Only some people can draw in those crowds
Those people have art that should speak to everyone
Most is close enough
The smaller crowds are equally intriguing
They're more vulgar and demeaning
Just like the artists they came to see
Niche, taboo, occult
Opinions that insult and complicate
Opinions abound share this awkward space
And draw crowds... even mine?
That's dreadful

anyone but you

Leave me alone, please
I know I need to be saved
I'd rather die then

you have a flare for treachery

Trust you? Yes, I do
This knife in my back's not yours
We are alone here

amends

Apology
Atonement
Quittance of pride
Restitution to avoid retribution
What I said
Shouldn't have been said
What I did
Should have never been done
I have shown you the worst of me
Naked emotion, unbounded
Raw and disgusting
You will know what you've always sought
What you see
My love is yours
Thank you

mirage

Perceptions are what are real
And I perceive that the associations you chose
Define you
That asshole right there, your friend
Only reveals
That you're an asshole too
A person I would never defend
I don't care about your different lives
When you're far apart
Your agreements is where your wily friendship starts
And that is my concern
That this is your life
Your life and your heart
My advice spurns
A natural descent
Make sure your time with friends is better spent
With better friends earned
That is horrible to learn

onliest

When I thought I was alone
I thought I was happy
Alone
No one here, kill me please
I'm too happy
Why am I this happy?
Because I'm alone
No one is here, hooray!
This is not how I felt yesterday

you're not supposed to be walking

Order! Order must be established
Accomplishments must be measured in steps
You can't get to the next step without that climb
An arduous climb from a previous, less difficult step
Which only prepares you for another more wearisome step
Every step must be acknowledged, it must
Your knees must endure experience pure
This I order!
Absolutely, this is the vestige of effort
Crawl! Get on your knees and crawl!
Stop walking!

digger

You've dug a hole for yourself
Wide and deep, very deep
You dig and dig, you've dug
And you have no clue why
This hole isn't your grave
Or your home
You just keep digging
Against your responsibilities and health
You just keep digging
Against your heart, your will
You want out the hole, to stop digging
But it's automatic, measured, metered
You can't drop the shovel

the preventative measures to ensure that you behave

They worked!
Well, I'll be damned!
They too now believe that every interaction must be planned
I can't understand how these monsters can't see that they've only harassed
Not just one or two, more than 100 people crass
Everyone, every single one was a desperate jerk
But again, they worked!
No one says anything to anyone anymore
Public interactions don't have to be ignored
All the shame of raw expression
Is not even suppressed
Or irked
It isn't shown and this is how it should be
Everyone shows respect by saying nothing at all
No one has to answer because no one calls
I can go about my day without any unneeded disruptions
Don't talk to me, it disturbs how I function
Don't say anything to me!
Don't look at me, don't smell me, just hide
If I fall, I'm glad you won't tell me my shoes were untied

america's most complete poet

"So many poets he's read
Every form he's mastered and bettered
While creating his own forms
That will survive the annals of the ages
He will be studied and pondered
And scholars will pontificate and swoon
Over every poem, every line, every syllable
His epics, his general prose will be worshipped
Every corner a t-shirt with his face
Musicians and painters will interpret him
The English language has never had a better penman
A daring daring artist… Only Shakespeare has been as competent
Jonathan Sheppard has been the voice we all lack"
Who the fuck is that?

my heart the drum

Sight is a curse
When I look upon your beauty
I seriously, truly, indignantly hurt
Every gaze, newly
Makes my heart beat with the harm
Of a drummer with no arms

you better vote!

Today is election day
So you know your duty
As a citizen of the United States
You must vote! For not voting is unruly

It doesn't matter if you know the candidate
Or the issues
Just vote dammit!
You're not American if you refuse

I voted yes on Proposition 19
It enacts a law
That won't allow for people mean
Happiness is all that needs to be saw

In a landslide the will to be happy wins!
There will be no more grief, dejection, or misery
Now if any action saddens
In jail you'll be
For you need to feel lucky
Today is the day that distress and sorrow did end

misanthrope

Why was I even there?
You invited me and you know how I am
I only exist to hate you, and them? I rue!
And that's exactly why you care

Even if it's a sham
You breathe the lust I spew
I exhale all I love to share
I despise you and everyone, fuck y'all! I don't give a damn!

Actually, I'll be honest, coy, and true
I am no heir
I am hate's beginning; it's birth, its scam
It's awful and harrowing cue

Oh your despair
Another pointless and futile attempt, grand
There is nothing you could ever do!
I will never care!
About you...
Or any other person no matter their height, size, or mind
See you next time

lord of the flies

There are many flies
There are millions of damn flies
I'm faster than them

what can you do?

You, you, you, you, you, you, you, you
What can you do?
It's always about you! Never about me!
What can I do?
It's about you, you, you, you, you, you, you
You, you, you, you, you, you, you, you, you, you
You, you, you, you, you, you, you, you
You, you, you, you, you, you, you
You, you, you, you, you, you
You, you, you, you, you
I can do nothing
You don't want to

why we've moved digital

You know why we've moved digital?
Do you truly know?
Let me ask a different question
Do you know why there is a big push to move digital?
To abandon print, to forget it, and "save trees"
Sanity expresses that it's a new age
Where we must save the trees?
So we could breathe in the future
But guess why we did it? Why humanity in all of our valor
Decided to save trees, the planet
The printed word
Read a word on a Kindle
Then read that word written on a piece of paper
Read a word on your smart phone
Then read that word printed in a magazine
Read any word from your computer
Then read those same words in a newspaper
Visceral and dense and unyielding
They exist where your body dwells
And aren't simply a figment of your "online" experience
The printed word is cold
And hits you with a haymaker in your heart
It makes you shiver and freeze
I hope you've heeded these words
I hope you've read them

29 Years Later...

I can only imagine the agony on my mother's face
She saw another after the initial
My beautiful brother's cries, followed five minutes later
By my cries
The first cry I remember, so agonizing
And here I am 29 years later
I won't speak for him, my twin
I never could and never would
29 years later
I'm struggling to stop crying
I was left behind for those five minutes
That eternity
Those last minutes
All those nutrients I enjoyed
And continue to indulge
The last born
The curse
The one who you didn't mean to be born
29 years later, still enjoying what isn't mine
29 years later, still designed
To count time and lies
29 years later here I am
29 years later still wishing I wasn't
29 years later understanding I had to be
29 years later saying what I thought wasn't true
29 years later I owe
What 29 years earlier devotes
A life of hubris, troublesome
Nobody if nobody was someone

you're going to die anyway

I might as well eat all of this food at once
I should probably taste all of this food now
Let me do all the drugs I can
All of the drugs
High and low and buried
I should play with the Lions
High and crazy
I should fraternize with Lions in a Gazelle's disguise, high
I should swim when I can't

i love your theory

What is that you said?
I agree! That is wrong to do
I have never heard anyone articulate as well
Why this practice, that occurrence is wrong
Everyone knows that is wrong
And everyone knows it's wrong because it absolutely is
I can't believe it happened again!

#activism

FUCK THE POLICE, HARD!
THEY ABUSE OUR TRUST! WHY? HOW?
THIS TREND MUST DIE NOW!
TAKE MY PICTURE, PLEASE?
IN FRONT OF THIS BURNING CAR
For my Twitter feed

altruism

Noble
How noble you are
The welfare of others is your greatest concern
And for that, you are noble
So humane!
No... you're all heart, a good heart
A philanthropic bleeding heart
Only here and only alive to care
Generous and considerate
No other soul is as noble
You're not kind for taxes
You're not kind to feel better about yourself
You're not kind, but magnanimous
An altruistic spirit
There needs to be more people like you
I wonder why there isn't?
Maybe...
It's the existence of people like me
That find futility
In your nobility

frame

What a moment!
Captured perfectly
This picture worth only one word
Look how happy she is
No... her mouth is about to open
She looks surly
Or maybe she looks disturbed
That's what I insist
Disturbed, the only word spoken
And surely
All the picture meant to unearth
Is that "disturbed" must exist
Broken

if you've never thought of death, you always should have

And that's why you protect your family
You stand there stoic
Scared but prepared
But your family can't know it
Your family can't know that you're scared to die
And even more scared of their demise
Because then you'll have to leave
Because you're selfish
And because you can't live without them
Now I knew I would only die
That's all I could ever do
But my family must live forever
And I must protect that!
I drive
And a wheel's crash
My family is okay
I'm okay
But we're frayed
All thoughts on our son
All fear that turned to anger on each other
And how we couldn't protect each other
And our son
Death happens out of nowhere
It can't be planned or planned for
There is no middle age
And you can't die too young
It is what happens to us
...to life as we know it
I cannot wait to be
That person that lives for eternity

#symbiosis

Walking through the Mall
Everyone is looking at me
Look at how I walk
What I am wearing, I am royalty
Impeccable, fashion forward, and trendy
All those days in the gym
Are what my beauty has come to be
This is what I envisioned
I am a sculpter, a molder
I am a sculpture
Look at everyone looking at me
And they're taking pictures too
Just to remember me
They're taking video
To remember my walk
I'm a star... stopped
I have hundreds of thousands following me
They really like me...
No... they love me!
They want to wear what I'm wearing
"Asshole you're holding up the line...
Your selfie is going to make me miss the movie time."
Don't you rush me, peon! I am...
Only taking a picture for my Instagram

caution: realities crossing

Conflict always arises down here
One man from one life
Crosses paths with another man from one other life
Both have one but together none
They claim the road because their experience resides
In a prism that they couldn't imagine another one sharing
It is a petulant encounter, pettish and then violent

A woman and her beauty and vitality
Crosses paths down here with another woman
Both ideal and alluring, resplendent
If equality existed, they'd be equally enchanting
But both only know the superiority
Of the lives they lived, theirs, the only one
Both consumed by the compulsion to conquer

She owns the crossing and so does she
He has dibs on the crossing and so does he
The grandest place where realities meet
A dirt road meets with a brick road
Which intersects a granite road
Roads of cement, cobblestone, and grass
Roads of silver and gold

Travelled by bicycle, buggy, horseback
Travelled by every vehicle bound to the ground, any mode desired
All end down here, this crossing which is now a graveyard
Empty cars and trucks, dead horses, and bike wheels
Make great tombs and tombstones for the prideful
All of the travelers who never recognized and despised
All realities not in their purview, their imagination, their guise

Here they lie
And that's the reality I surmise
Now leave my crossing or it is here where you'll die
Here where you'll lie
This way I own
All alone
Leave mine and return home

the censor ship

Your order is here
It arrived on shore today
I can't unload it

"do you swear to tell the truth, so help you god?"

"Hold up your right hand
Do you swear to tell the truth
Do you swear to tell the whole truth
On this stand
This sanctuary of truth
This absolute infallible beacon of truth
Under the one omniscient, omnipotent god?
If you lie, immediately you'll die
Instantaneously your credibility will be lost
And promptly you'll be tossed
Into a chasm of loss
You better not lie
In god's name to hell you'll be damned
Because the truth soothes
All it does is soothe"
Damn god, goddamn it!
What if I hate this supposed sleuth?
This universal spy, loose
Equate his lies with truth? God is off
If god represents infallibility I should die
Right here, right now on this stand
Before the judge and the jury, all of humanity
Because if it is god's honest truth
That you want from me
You'll never get it, honestly

you have a good heart in there

Think happy thoughts
The thoughts that should always be thought
A good heart should always be sought
Never succumb to those bad thoughts
Never believe those days of darkness
Begrudge them, disclaim and disavow them
For all hearts are meant to be good I stress
Hearts were never meant to endure murkiness
Or its sin
Smiles and blooming flowers, laughter
Experience and its glowing chapters
Happiness after the rapture
All the glee captured
This is what life is all about
Forget pain, and suffering, fuck agony
Fuck agony, no doubt
Fuck the pangs of affliction, its rout
That's not life, that is phony
Think happy thoughts
The thoughts that should always be thought
A good heart should always be sought
Never succumb to those bad thoughts
Black is the good heart
Because it denied those hearts dark

anonymous source

"He is too awful!"
"No one likes him. He sucks!"
said Anonymous

xq (nathaniel's first poem)

wu;;;;;;;;;;lp-
p=============================pp====================pp,,,,,,,,,,,,,,,,pp,===,,,,,,,,,,,,,,,,============ddqdp==][[qo\\[\\\\\\\,000000,s'kl;kp[[[[[[[[[[[[[[[[[[[[kp-;,0=kk

the lexicon: modern language

One word was added to the lexicon today
Most would define it this way

1.) A self-righteous, moralist ass hole
Who only sees 'me' in the whole

2.) A person incapable of being wrong or defective
A dolt elected

3.) Someone stinking, base and ignoble
Humanities foible

4.) A bastard moron
An awful song

You better not ever use this word against me
Those things I can never be!
Fuck you, and your claim
That this word is my name

ugly hatred

I'm not attracted
You are ugly, I'm sorry
And I hate ugly

the self-indulgence of satire

Offense taken!
Why do you think what you think about me,
I should accept as a joke?
You call me defiant
Because I deny your comedic license
Why do you find it necessary to prod and poke
All of my sensibilities?
You are sadly mistaken

I'm not going to laugh or understand
What you find funny
Stop trying to make me laugh
I'm not going to accept everyone's pleasantry
Of thinking of me as drollery
You know what's bad?
About you calling me a dummy
You think that's all I am
Even worse, there
For some reason I care

tarnation

Oh, Hell!
Isn't this place swell?
I love the warmth

hindsight

The past is clear to me now
I got that wrong
So much I would have done differently
It wasn't that bad
I wasn't that sad
I'm sadder now

i hate disneyland

I've never been to Disneyland
But I hate it
Truly, I hate it
It doesn't make any sense to me
I know its escapism
And how we should escape

This completely fabricated universe
A reality created by a man and his corrupt team
Transfixed in irrational bliss...
"Who ruined your childhood?
You must have had a sad childhood.
Who doesn't love Disneyland?"

Who is the one still trying to relive their youth?
Now, this is me being my most cynical
Why is it a big deal?
Why can't I just go to Disneyland and have a good time?
Why can't I just go to Tokyo, or Hong Kong, or Paris
And enjoy their Disneyland?

Why can't I traverse the Disncy world?
Why can't I enjoy it for my love?
Why can't I have an amazing time for my son?
How can I hate somewhere I've never been?
A destination with rave reviews
A place that creates no frowns

Where sorrow drowns
It may be because I've never had time
Or maybe I'm not fond of Disney movies
Or music and the reality they create
The lessons and beliefs and love they force us to believe
The tragedy that always creates worth and purpose

I hate the formula Disney devised for happiness
I hate that happiness is always an escape
And not what is
"Hi, Mickey!"

afflated

I never thought I'd write again
For weeks I think they were
For months it could have been
Words weren't here
I'm writing because of you
You

fuck that fuck

Fuck that fucking fuck!
That fucker is not shit… shit!
Stupid, sad, fucker

compliance

Deference is my reference
Docility is my liability
Obedience is my reverence
Oddly it is also my tranquility

Good god I only obey
I am very hush
And only say
What I am beholden to, what's rushed

I cooperate
I refuse to hate
Easily I conform
I love the norm

Fucking fuck why do I listen?
Is she always right?
Are her wishes fruition?
Or unfulfillment's right...

I'm tired of listening to you
This is the last time I listen to you, true
Your desires I will no longer own
Leave me the fuck alone
Please?!

futility

What haven't I tried?
Every attempt frivolous
Maybe this will work

you're not happy and i know it

"Why are you doing that?
Why are you doing this?
Why can't you always do what I want you to?
Why do you have your own free will?
Why can't you feel how I feel?
Why? Why? Why?
Why aren't you happy with me?
Because you want to be free?
You're never going to be free!
You're never going to be happy
You need to learn to accept that
You can be anything except that
I will ensure you will never be happy
You'll always be wishin'
For volition"

self-determined

I have some power?
Not a little, but a lot?
I need to use this

a new idea

It has been centuries since a new idea has emerged
That is incredible
Solely amazing
Intelligence borrows ideas
And genius steals them
I believe geniuses are stupid
For how are you intelligent
If you only extrapolate from a template?
Anyone can do that
And it's only thought to be genius
If what you deduce is understood
Genius is what has never been thought
Then pulled into existence
From a muse that can't be discerned
What if we stopped thinking?
Now that's not a new idea
Many people never think, ever
And never will
Benumbed by unremitting thoughts of new forms
New forms that already exist
How the fuck do I invent something new?
The vastness of my mind
An infinity of possibilities and all have been traversed
Where will I find this new idea?
Why can't I succeed where all of the geniuses failed?
Because I'm dumber than them, I'm a goddamned idiot

in a bottle lost

I always knew the cost
More than the price at the register
My health and my family's well-being lost
This elixir so strong and fair
Sobriety always fought
I may never get there

follow

Walk with me
Follow, follow
March with me
Follow, follow
Believe with me
Follow, follow

I have the answers
That you never sought
Follow my thoughts
Believe my interpretation
Believe its cancer
Embrace your fascination

Walk with me
Follow, follow
March with me
Follow, follow
Believe with me
Follow, follow

Follow with me
How to buy
Follow how I think or try
To no end
Follow, you'll be trendy
Follow and don't pretend

Walk with me
Follow, follow
March with me
Follow, follow
Believe with me
Follow, follow

You won't be relevant
Are you thinking?
You have a mind shrinking
Seeking
You aren't elegant?
I had this inkling

Walk with me
Follow, follow
March with me
Follow, follow
Believe with me
Follow, follow

Following is your predilection
I won't punish you for that
In fact
Where should I begin?
You must follow, even if it's fiction
Lead? You can't, a growing trend

pleasure trends...

You know what I like?
And what I love to do best?
The same things as you

advocates

Champion a cause
That's what my words always say
My actions say lose

listless

I have something I
Want to say, wanna hear it?
You sure? ... I want out

support system

"What do you believe is the corner stone of your success?
Who helped you become the person you are today?"
Forgive me for saying this, or don't, but
That's a fucked up question
"What about that question do you detest?"
I disagree that anyone had a say
In anything about me but my DNA
If I'm in a rut
Why is that alone, my obsession?
My "support system" didn't blunder?
When I am considered "successful"
They are my catalyst, this ordained stimulant
"I feel that you still don't understand yourself
Your perception and the reality around you are asunder
What person wants to support your thoughts, stressful?
Your disposition detestable?
This life is about absolution and resilience
You hate yourself, you can't accept someone's worth or wealth"

I devalue life? I don't appreciate breath or our lungs?
I am awful because I contend
That if there are people "responsible" for your success
Then in your failure they're also culpable?
You should be hung!
If you think that is dumb
How can you defend
"Friends, family, and supporters" who suggest
That what you're inclined to do is despicable?

They refuse to support you or acknowledge you
Even worse they refute your beliefs
Friends and family that only allow you to assume
"Friends and family" that only know your good days
Who know and refute
What you eat
Despite it being their favorite treat
"So you're denying your own doom?
You don't believe in a brace, or what they would say?"

I don't, all this means to me
Is that not many support me
And not only because I don't ask
It isn't a noble task

intents and purposes

It is my intensive purpose
To not speak for all volition
I will not qualify my intentions
Certainty is my surface
Why mire in practicality?
In your statement you're hoping
That most thought is soaking
In your sea of discernment and morality
Say what you mean
Don't speak for me
Don't speak for them or some base essence, horribly
Speak with a confidence obscene
This is the only allegory
That one should redeem

unlawful detainer: get the fuck out now!

I don't care if you
Have the rent, the money to pay
You're not welcome here

moving with time

Time can't measure me
I'm not young and I'm definitely not old
I just am
Newness is me
I am reborn over and over and over
Every second I am born
I can't grow old
And wouldn't know how if I could

he is me

She wants him to be
Like the father he won't meet
It would always be

my first and last poem about seattle

The platitudes about the city of my birth, from them I'll try to refrain
For they surely inform my disposition dejected
Overcast, this constant unceasing overcast
A place where the sun always loses to the clouds' pain
The only agony the city respected
Because it seems to always last
For the rest of my life I want to always prepare
For cloudless air

I don't want to see a single cloud in the sky
Drought stricken, drought ridden, who cares?
I don't want to see one drop of rain
For all that means is one less day in my inane life's lie
Without the glory of the sun's stare
I respect what water brings and how without it life is lame
But those drops on my head
Make me want to be dead

"It rains a lot in Seattle, doesn't it."
Maybe it does, I haven't been there in a long time
I stay away, because I don't want to know
When I was there the rain was incidental, it was wit
The rain was with time aligned
I awoke and went to bed soaked and low
And never thought that the rain ruled my feelings
I never understood the power that the clouds were wielding

Gray and white skies weren't forever there
I remember the sunny summers, and the rainbows the rain brought
The puddles that came the same, where the rainbows ended
As a youth I splashed and splashed and splashed without care
And each color of the rainbow was a slide bought
Traveled down and crashed into a time splendid
I am proud to be from a town owned by gloom
Even if it means peril in a town built on the sun's doom

It's my past that I hate
To claim that my animus for the city of my birth
Only belongs to something as incidental as the weather

Is similar to a fool believing scripture's bait
And how they find my depreciating worth
In how they understand that I'm crazy, and how I'll never be better
Seattle! Seattle! Seattle! I love you forever
Even if never living there again makes me better

justification

I like this because
It is the right thing to like
My heart says it is

incidence

There are incidents and there is incidence
Recently I wrote that incidence is almost inconsequential
That the weather shouldn't affect how we maneuver
But that was me being my most foolish
How can I order myself to deny
Happenstance?
There is no reconciling the free will of others
You get in your car and drive in the same direction as some asshole
You'll never know
That day can be the day where you drift together
Forever marred by contact you had never thought or planned
How can my mood and its druthers not be moved
By the sun and her warmth
Or her insufferable days of anger where she attempts to melt
Everything
If all of my intentions are drowned by Biblical floods
Or if the city is enduring the last days of the Ice Age,
What if winds are wearying the hat on my head,
And its blown into traffic and a car runs over my hat,
Wet from the rain soaked pavement
My hat left and forgotten under the ice and frost
Then faded and scarred by the noonday sun?
The incidents in experience still, only happenstance
Maybe I didn't have to wear the hat
I knew what the weather could do to my head
My hat just a casualty of a futile war
Against preparing for what you cannot control
It isn't my fault if I get angry or sad or even happy
I can't control anything!

desperation

Anything, right now!
Please! Anything, I beg you
To save me from this

i see the light hiding

Light is the universe's greatest anomaly
It should be yearned for
Because it is rare
Light brings life and uncovers the bare
Danger is no where around when light is near
The preponderance of darkness
Its likelihood rules existence
When I blink
I only fear never opening my eyelids again
And enjoying when they don't

do you know where you are?

Your hubris almost, almost makes me forget where I am
I'm not the most stable person
Retreats into complete disregard of verity I attend
More than very often
But you seem to dwell there
I'm not judging you
Maybe I'm the one who doesn't know what's up
Or what's down or what's all around
Maybe I don't see
That this isn't reality

demolitionist

A laborious job
What else could it be?
It's arduous and dangerous
But spiritedly I build
Every nut and bolt tight and tough
The best steel, stone, and craftsmanship are this pathway
Ensured by me; the contractor, the architect, the builder
And confidence in this new union
Over troubled waters
At the bottom of a jagged canyon
Formed supremely, without spite and with concord
This bridge, the ease of access to our communion
I must burn to the ground

not you too

Insecurity is a plague that eats at me
All I do and write was born in Hell's dregs
That is my claim alone and aura of my environment
And I refuse to chastise those who are paralyzed
At Hell's legs

What I do and say and write can be a disease
And all I've made
Is how my heart, mind, and thoughts went
And also how the hearts, minds, and time influenced were sterilized
I am not afraid

Maybe I write because I like being lonely
And uncherished is how I was meant to age
But to tell me that all of the time I spent
Trying to keep myself from wanting to die
Were years, months, weeks, hours, minutes, seconds, a-waste

Is something I cannot fathom, adumbrate or see
Blinded by your false love and support I was, lost in your maze
I believed that you believed, you don't and you didn't
That would have never been a surprise
If I weren't in love's lustful daze

I understand your needs
Security is what you crave
Without hard work's boundless and unrelenting sentence
I will work hard for as long as I am alive
Until my dying day coming soon, I will never believe
That you believed in me
Because you didn't
You didn't, you couldn't

humanity ingénue

A seed implanted in a woman
Artless and combative
Without a similar woman
I wouldn't be here
Astral and dull

judge, jury, executioner, and mortician

I am a true model of existence
So live like me
I am not vain or materialistic
I live a life of substance
Of deep human inquiry
I refuse to be a statistic
So I hate those who do
What I would never do
And live how I wouldn't live too
That I can't forgive

But maybe they're right
Maybe worship of idols who create
Items more than most find desirable
Is art, and righteous. Whose might
Is built strong and art's fate
Maybe I shouldn't find laughable
How they interpret what they see
How they tend to be
Or what they find comfy
Facts have to be my guide

I am correct!
That manner of living
Fails next to what is natural to me
I don't know what you expect
But your choices and your life are unforgiving
And for all of your trespasses, constantly
You must die!
You know why?
Because your standard of life
Was something that I've decided to be wrong

How satisfying it was
To get rid of you, a free thinker
A revolutionary and rebel
All those ways of living found superfluous
Is why humanity whimpers
You didn't think like my mind expels
So I had to bury you
Because how you live isn't true
For the benefit of death's due
You had to be embalmed

doo doo monster

Son, why did you do that?
You might as well have shit on me
You almost destroyed your inheritance
I'll change your diaper faster next time

there is only one way to go from here

I hope what they say
About being here is true
I'm on my way up

"i've got some soul searchin' to do"

Come out!
I'm tired of lookin'
This unwanted game of hide 'n seek
Did I choose to play?
Who am I looking for?
What am I looking for?
I never thought to look before
My ignorance didn't explore
And won't lay
With this demented game for the desperate and bleak
Am I lookin' for a spookin'?
Or for a morality devout?
Come out, come out! I will find you
That hole, that I should have
Come out, come out and let's laugh
And rue
That I believed there was a path
All I want is a soul to boast
Either the soul doesn't exist or mine is a ghost

abaddon

How did I get here?
This place I have always feared
Lost all along trying to find
A place kind
I've been looking for an exit
And goddamn it I can't find it
There must be a world, a universe nicer
A realm not overwhelmed by fire
Or the detestation of me
And all that I believe
A fascinating sphere that isn't so hot
Here, I refuse to rot
This land isn't for me, no one here is warm
I hate that this terrible place is where I was born

control locus

No matter the weather
The bodies that surround me
And their free will
Don't make me worse or better
There is nothing, no entity that can incite
Or make me move needlessly
My actions, like my reaction still
When the sun is up, I sleep
The moon gives me energy
Outside and inside
My thoughts perceive me
Every leap is me
Every leap astounds
And inside me resides
A focus that can only see
That all of my control resides in me

chairman of the bored

What to do, what to do?
What do I want to do today?
Chores?
Bore
Exercise?
Why?
Read?
Please!
Write?
Yeah right...
What to do, what to do?
What do I do right now?
At this very moment...
Besides sit down

societal ills

I'm not responsible for my environment
I was born and I have life
Who birthed me sucks
Where I live is fucked
How can I control what I didn't create?
How can I change it too?
Should I be like them over there?
The rich or those who've had the privilege
To not be molested or poor
Those who can eat what and whenever they want?
I should always want and have a secure roof
My parents should love each other, still
And one or both should have never died
That's how it should be? That's how I should be?
I am hard, I am troublesome and hurt-filled
And it isn't my fault goddamn it!
I know I am
And what I am
It isn't my fault
Society is to blame
I am this way without choice

the trauma of childhood

It would be odd
If my youth were different
My current life I laud
Because, maybe I like me, maybe

you are not a poet

You know you're not a poet
Come on you dumb motherfucker
Lil' Wayne is more of a poet than you
Drake is more of a poet than you
Gucci Mane is a great poet
But I'm not
Neither is he
They aren't either
Fuck all that, no poems have ever been written
Only words
Words and phrases, thoughts and letters
Written well against awful's discriminate disregard
You're not a poet
You are human
What's a "human?"
A poet
And I'm a miscreation
Subhuman

morality's legislators

I've caught you asshole!
This red-light finds you guilty
I will never hide
I am honest like the lens
And will not abide
By rules that make you my judge
You are mistake free
Behind your lens free to judge
You capture all wrong
You are a foolish fool, wrong
To think that you sin
Less than those in the center
Of your worth, your lens
Point your camera at you

mistakes were made

Yeah I believe lies
"Working hard yields success" LIES
I don't want to work

the will of ambition

I desire success badly
How do I define great accomplishment?
What do I consider progress?
I don't know sadly
Maybe, I think it's easily paying my rent
Unburdened by money's stress

What I love to do I want to do forever
To write and create and sit and think
I want to play with my son, teach him, grow with him
Wishful thoughts that will be, never
That's not what I should preach or to my being link
But the prospect of financial independence seems grim

That is my will
Not to have to deal with the need for money
For my autonomy to rely upon a structure
Whose purpose, whose will
Is to corrupt, exploit, and destroy, simply
That is where my ambition must go, my being ruptured

The will of ambition
Is to protect and love my family
The will of ambition truly
Is to hate and destroy other families nutrition
And damn me...
If I engage in that practice... fully

ambiguity's reason

Reason is the greatest fight to be fought
There is some lesson here, there has to be
Why else would what happened have happened?
Why lie in action...
When there is something of value to retrieve?
That's what I thought
Experience has taught me to never trust
And I could never have confidence
In definitions that aren't defined
I'm sorry but clarification is sublime
Explain to me your confused deference
Or hush
The fence between us two
I didn't think you'd walk so tightly
I boo
Your ambiguous thoughts mightily

why bad thoughts?

Bad thoughts aren't uncommon
In fact, I have experienced them more often than those thoughts good
Or those thoughts of good
Well... those thoughts I have been taught are supposed to be good
Originally, I believed that bad thoughts were subjective
Like why should I think a sunrise or sunset are beautiful?
And why is that bad?
Why is empathy lauded and obsessed over?
Care and good, being nice and genial, gracious
Are traits of a good human being
You can demonize me, of course you can, will, and do
Because sunsets and sunrises are poo
Bad thoughts is the refuge for those who can't and never would
Force themselves to think other than they do
Influence rules us all
We aren't Adam or Eve
Or the first organism that began evolution
But those who deny bad things, bad hearts, bad souls
Seem to be people who invented good
Those who have done bad things
Think bad thoughts
Have bad hearts
Were born with bad souls
Think that what you think is awful
For those who think that sunsets are drudgery
For those who know that the sun is evil
And rises only to cause worriment
They also hate the moon because it's light
Is owned by the sun
What they covet is blindness
Those bad thoughts that look straight into the sun
To achieve that goal
Myopia, a defect that should be cheered
Because it champions that cause and the direction of your head in the sky

well-adjusted

I don't think I'm bad
And I know that I'm not evil
I'm not a demon or a devil
I'm just being all I ever had
I acknowledge the upheaval
I look how evil looks, I bedevil

"I think it is simply because of your mask
That is supposed to be a demon
And you know it is too
You know what they'll ask
They being those interested in your reason
Do you read what you write, and know what you do?"

Of course, I'm not surprised
I am aware of the prejudices against my face
I won't deny or hide from them
And I have no scheme to devise
I do not bask in my disgrace
I am not hiding because hiding has no end

"So you believe that you're well adjusted?
You're not evil or defined by the stupid mask you're wearing?
Not many people walk around wearing the mask of a demon
They wear the face for which they were thrusted
You pretend to be uncaring
But you're still hiding behind vanity's treason!"

Do not thrust your judgment upon me
I am not insane, this is my surface
Is my face, my heart?
My soul is defined vile because I'm ugly?
That's what your thoughts preface?
That's why I'm marked?

"That is not a mask. Your face, you're wearing?
You're saying that you were born with horns?
You're not lying, you're not hiding?
This truth you're marrying
To your life sworn
Is that you're hideous and you didn't do the deciding?"

This is who I am, goddamn it!
Do I judge you? Or give a fuck about your beauty?
I am who? I am? I am what I say, and then what I do!
"You don't have to throw a fit."
Yes, I fucking do! It's getting harder for you people to see
I am well adjusted, I am not crazy, no matter your view

about the author

Jonathan Sheppard is a Seattle born writer, based in Los Angeles. He primarily writes cynical, brooding, dark, and angstsy introspective poetry that occasionally delves into a macro understanding of self and society but he also writes similarly themed essays and short stories. Jonathan has a Bachelor's degree in English from UCLA. He has written three books of poetry, and one book of short stories, *Bad Stories*.

INSTAGRAM: @iamjonathansheppard
EMAIL: chiefjonny@badthoughtspublishing.com
WEBSITE: http://www.jonathansheppard.org

works cited

baudrillard, jean. ch. 5 *cool memories*. paris. ed. galilee. 1990. print.

huxley, aldous. *time must have a stop*. new york: harper & bros., 1994. print.

www.ingramcontent.com/pod-product-compliance
Lightning Source LLC
Chambersburg PA
CBHW081207170426
43198CB00018B/2882